People of Destiny

A Humanities Series

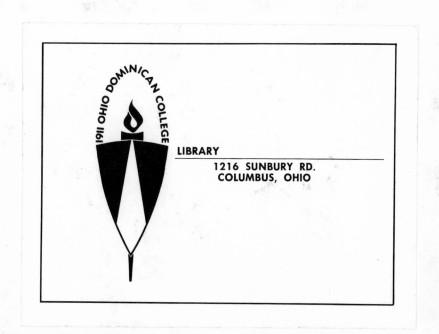

1911 OHIO DOMINICAN COLLEGE

LIBRARY

1216 SUNBURY RD.
COLUMBUS, OHIO

There comes a time,
we know not when,
that marks
the destiny of men.

Joseph Addison Alexander

People of Destiny

ELEANOR ROOSEVELT

By Kenneth G. Richards

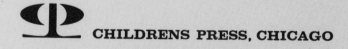 CHILDRENS PRESS, CHICAGO

*The editors wish to express
their appreciation to Mr. Meyer Goldberg,
who created the series and inspired
the publication of* People of Destiny.

Cover and body design: John Hollis

Project editor: Joan Downing

Assistant editor: Elizabeth Rhein

*Illustrations: Harley Shelton—Hollis
Associates*

Research editor: Robert Hendrickson

*Photographs: From the files of Wide
World Photos, Inc.*

Typesetting: American Typesetting Co.

Printing: Regensteiner Press

Contents

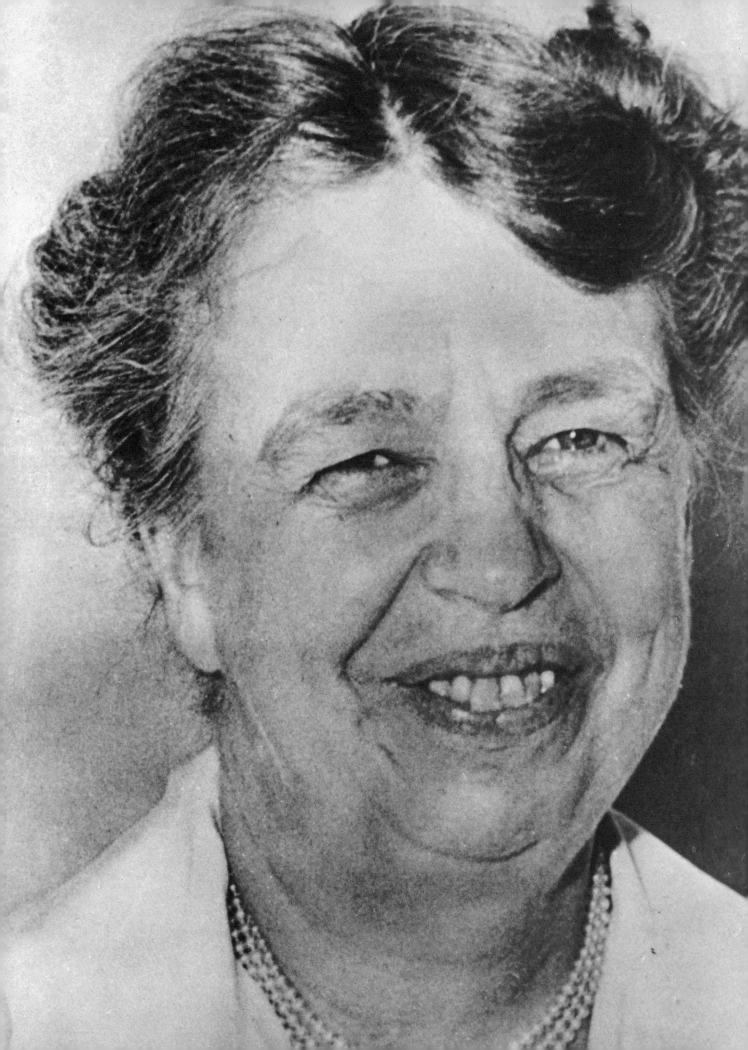

A Champion for Human Rights

On a chilly day in December of 1945, Eleanor Roosevelt and a few of her friends were having lunch in her New York apartment on Washington Square when the telephone rang. Excusing herself from her guests, she left the room to answer it. She was surprised to hear President Harry Truman's voice. She was even more surprised to hear him ask her to serve as a member of the American delegation to the United Nations, which was being organized at that time.

Her first reaction was to decline, for she felt that her background and experience did not qualify her to fill such an important position. Mr. Truman persisted, however, and finally Mrs. Roosevelt said that she would consider it carefully and let him know her answer soon.

Eight months had passed since the untimely death of her husband, President Franklin Delano Roosevelt. It had been a very busy eight months for the widow. First, there had been the sad, harrowing days of making burial arrangements and then the impressive funeral at the family home in Hyde Park, New York. After more than twelve years in the White House, collecting all the Roosevelt belongings and moving to New York had been a tremendous chore. Then came the long procedure of settling Mr. Roosevelt's estate.

Yes, they had been eight long months, but at last Mrs. Roosevelt had settled into a new way of life and had already begun to cast about for some form of meaningful endeavor. She was well-off financially, and could have spent the rest of her days in easy luxury. There was a restless spirit in Eleanor Roosevelt, however, that made retirement impossible. She had a deep concern for the welfare of others. She cared deeply about discrimination, political repression, famine, poverty, and disease and as long as these continued in the world, she could not rest if there was any way she could fight them.

Perhaps she would be able to make a meaningful contribution as a delegate to the United Nations. She confided the President's offer to a few friends and relatives. All urged her to accept. Still she had her doubts, for she felt that someone with more experience could do a better job and thereby make a greater contribution. Her friends told her not to worry, and reminded her that the State Department would conduct briefings for all the delegates before the General Assembly actually met in London. Besides, they said, she would be lending the prestige of the Roosevelt name to the American delegation.

Eleanor continued to think it over. As an orphan child, she had been filled with fears and doubts about her capabilities. As she matured, however, she had gained confidence, and in time these fears and doubts disappeared. Only major decisions occasionally brought them fleetingly back to bother her. "In my early married years," she wrote in her autobiography, "the pattern of my life had been largely my mother-in-law's pattern. Later it was the children and Franklin who made the pattern." Now, for the first time in her life, Eleanor could make a decision without first having to consider how it would fit into someone else's pattern. This thought eased her dilemma a little, as did the fact that the decision involved service to others. A glowing compassion

for her fellow man was Eleanor Roosevelt's greatest motivating force. To lend assistance to someone in need, she could overcome all her fears. At last she made her decision and telephoned her answer to President Truman.

"I believed the United Nations to be the one hope for a peaceful world," she explained later. "I knew that my husband had placed great importance on the establishment of this world organization. At last I accepted in fear and trembling." The United States Senate quickly confirmed her nomination.

The first meeting of the United Nations General Assembly was held in London, England, early in 1946. Mrs. Roosevelt was assigned to Committee Three, which was concerned with humanitarian, educational, and cultural problems. Many considered this to be one of the least important committees, but as it turned out, one of the most controversial issues of the first meeting was generated in Committee Three.

In these first months after the end of World War II, there were millions of displaced persons living in temporary camps throughout Europe. Now that the war was over, the Russians and other Communist-dominated countries wanted these refugees to be shipped back to their native lands—forcibly if necessary. Most of these poor people did not want to return to live in their own countries under communism. Many, in fact, had openly opposed the Communists. The Russians, of course, wanted these people returned mainly

Refugees during World War II were sent to displaced persons' camps such as this one. They were forced to live there under squalid conditions until the United Nations determined that they could emigrate to the country of their choice.

to punish them by imprisonment or execution for their beliefs.

The American position was that each person should be able to choose freely where he wanted to go. Poles could return to Poland, Czechs to Czechoslovakia, and Russians to the U.S.S.R. if they so desired, but no one, the Americans felt, should be *forced* to return. After heated discussions, the question was finally to be put to a vote of the General Assembly. Speakers for each side were allowed time to present their cases before the assembly. The Russians chose their most impressive debater—the brilliant and much-feared Andrei Vishinsky. To present the Western point of view, the American delegation chose Mrs. Roosevelt.

"I said I would do my best," Mrs. Roosevelt wrote later. "I was badly frightened. I trembled at the thought of speaking against the famous Mr. Vishinsky."

This was a very important cause involving the safety and welfare of thousands of homeless refugees, however, and once again Eleanor Roosevelt overcame her fears in behalf of fellow human beings. She spoke with great charm and eloquence—though she had never been a noted speaker. She expressed America's cause with an honesty and a compassion that won the hearts—and votes—of many delegates from other nations. When the vote was tallied, it was overwhelmingly in favor of America's position. Displaced persons would have a choice.

Later that year, when the Human Rights Commission was formed, Eleanor Roosevelt was elected its chairman. She continued to be re-elected and held the post until 1951 when she resigned, feeling that the United States had held the chairmanship long enough.

As chairman of the Human Rights Commission, Mrs. Roosevelt could take tremendous satisfaction in seeing the Declaration of Human Rights through to completion. This instrument outlines the basic rights every human being should have under law. Most of these rights are taken for granted by Americans, but it took hard work and perseverance to make this declaration acceptable to many nations of vastly different social and economic conditions. During that five-year period, Mrs. Roosevelt worked unceasingly to see that everyone throughout the world would be able to enjoy the rights and freedoms outlined in the declaration.

Mrs. Roosevelt resigned from the United Nations delegation in 1952 to become the Chairman of the Board of Governors of the American Association for the United Nations. She was re-appointed as a delegate to the UN by President Kennedy in 1961, and upon her return the entire assembly rose when she entered. No other delegate has been so honored.

For years Eleanor Roosevelt had been an avowed enemy of racial and religious injustice in her own country. As America's first lady, she had fought unceasingly against poverty, intolerance, and prejudice. She had earned the everlasting affection of minority groups and the underprivileged.

Her ideals found new and broader meaning in the world forum of the United Nations. Millions of people around the world knew her name, heard her words, and gained new faith and hope for a better life. During her years as a delegate to the United Nations, Eleanor Roosevelt achieved a unique destiny. She became the world's foremost champion for human rights.

Above, Eleanor Roosevelt addresses the United Nations in her capacity as chairman of the Human Rights Commission. Top right, Mrs. Roosevelt grants an interview to high school students at the United Nations. Bottom right, Mrs. Roosevelt with John Foster Dulles, Secretary of State under President Eisenhower.

The Roosevelts of New York

In the year 1626, Peter Minuit purchased Manhattan Island in the Hudson River for sixty Dutch guilders—about twenty-four dollars. The brave and hopeful Dutch traders and colonists gave the struggling little settlement the imposing name of New Amsterdam. They hoped that the name would attract other settlers from Holland and that the community would grow. These pioneers could hardly imagine, however, that the little settlement on the edge of the wilderness would ever rival the great old city in Holland for which it was named.

Many settlers did come over from the "old country," among them a young man by the name of Claes Martensen van Rosenvelt who arrived in New Amsterdam in 1644 to make a new life for himself. He had no particular trade or profession, and he did not find much to his liking in the community. He pushed farther north along the Hudson River where he established a small farm. During the years that followed, Claes worked hard, raised a family, occasion-

ally fought off Indian attacks, and lived a life little different from the lives of other early colonists. He would have been forgotten to history but for one thing—he established the Roosevelt family in America. Two of Claes' descendants, Theodore and Franklin Roosevelt, would become presidents of the United States, at that time a union not even dreamed of by the most far-sighted men. Anna Eleanor Roosevelt, also a descendant, became known as the "First Lady of the World." These three would make the Roosevelt name a permanent part of American history.

It was Claes' son, Nicolas, who changed the spelling of the family name. Nicolas Roosevelt became a fairly well-to-do merchant and raised a large family of ten children. One of his sons, Jacobus, began the branch of the family that five generations later produced the thirty-second president of the United States—Franklin Delano Roosevelt. Another son, Johannus, was the direct ancestor of Theodore Roosevelt, the

Claes Martensen van Rosenvelt fights off an Indian attack near his farm, located up the Hudson River from New Amsterdam. He was the first member of the Roosevelt family to settle in the New World.

15

twenty-sixth president. Anna Eleanor Roosevelt was a sixth-generation descendant of Johannus.

When the English won control of the colony, New Amsterdam became New York but the various branches of the Roosevelt family still prospered through the years. Soon the Hudson Valley was dotted with their farms and estates. During the Revolutionary War, the Roosevelts, almost without exception, were patriots who fought for American independence. Roosevelts stood at the water's edge and watched Robert Fulton's steamboat, the *Clermont,* chug its way up the Hudson River on an historic day in 1807. In 1825, members of the Roosevelt clan witnessed the opening of the great Erie Canal connecting the Hudson River with the Great Lakes. As one of the oldest families in New York, the Roosevelts took pride in their state and an avid interest in its affairs.

Theodore Roosevelt was born in 1858 and his brother Elliott two years later. The future "Rough Rider" and hero of San Juan Hill was a sickly youth afflicted by frequent asthma attacks. Elliott, however, was a strong, athletic lad and an outdoorsman who loved hunting and riding. Their father stressed the need for physical activities and encouraged his sons in that direction. When he was only fifteen, Elliott went out to the frontier in Texas where he spent several months at an army outpost called Fort McKavit. He became an excellent shot with a gun and enjoyed hunting for wild game or skirmishing with hostile Indians.

The boys' father died suddenly when Elliott was still a teen-ager. Theodore went off to Harvard to continue his

Eleanor Roosevelt with her father, Elliott. Her father doted on her and affectionately called her "Little Nell," and though Eleanor rarely saw him, he became the "center of her world."

education, but Elliott used his inheritance money to finance a big-game hunting trip to Africa and India. He returned to New York to become the dashing hero of the social set. He was a handsome young man with a warm, outgoing personality that made him very popular.

Not long after his return to America, Elliott was asked by some distant cousins, James and Sara Roosevelt of Hyde Park, New York, to become the godfather of their newborn son. Elliott accepted the honor, and the baby—Franklin Delano Roosevelt—became his godson.

It was about this same time that Elliott met and fell in love with a striking dark-haired girl named Anna Hall, also a member of a socially prominent old New York family. One of her ancestors, Robert R. Livingstone, had served with Benjamin Franklin, John Adams, and Thomas Jefferson on the committee to draft the Declaration of Independence. Her family was quite wealthy and Anna was among the most beautiful young women in her social set. After a whirlwind courtship, Anna and Elliott were married in one of the big New York social affairs of the year 1883. They established residence in New York City, on Thirty-fourth Street, and on October 11, 1884, their first child was born. They named the baby Anna Eleanor.

Eleanor was to write years later, ". . . from all accounts I must have been a more wrinkled and less attractive baby than average. . . . " Nonetheless, she was the "apple of her daddy's eye" and he affectionately called her "Little Nell" after the character in Charles Dickens' *The Old Curiosity Shop*. "I never doubted," she added, "that I stood first in his heart."

The first few years of Eleanor's life were happy and lively. As with many wealthy families of that Victorian age, she saw relatively little of her parents except at prescribed times during the day. Her mother usually saw the children for a little while each afternoon. Eleanor and her baby brother, Elliott, Jr., spent the rest of the time with a nurse. Her beautiful mother was caught up in the social whirl of New York society, and her father spent much time at their country home in Hempstead, Long Island, hunting or playing polo. Each summer the children were sent to live with their Grandmother Hall at Tivoli-on-the-Hudson.

For all the family wealth, fine homes, lovely clothes, and servants, little Eleanor gradually became a lonely, unhappy child. She was never truly close to her mother, as most girls are. "My mother was troubled by my lack of beauty," she remembered, "and I knew it as a child senses these things. She tried hard to bring me up well so that my manners would compensate for my looks, but her efforts only made me more keenly conscious of my shortcomings."

Her father, on the other hand, thought she was a "miracle from Heaven." On several occasions, when he had a group of gentlemen friends in the house, Mr. Roosevelt showed off his little daughter. Dressed in her best finery, she would twirl and dance for the guests while her father beamed with delight. When her dance was through, her father would sit her high on his shoulders and carry her off to bed.

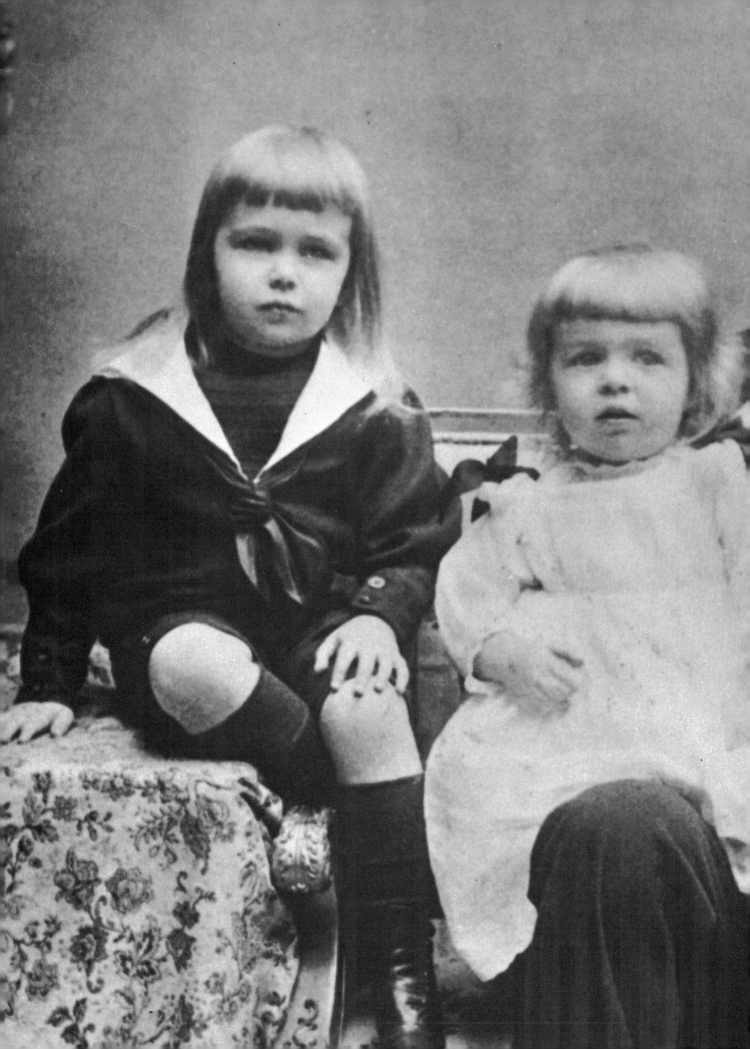

Elliott Roosevelt with his children. Left to right: Elliott, Jr., Hall, and Eleanor.

19

When Eleanor Roosevelt was six years old, her family decided to take a trip to Europe. After much fanfare and cries of Bon Voyage from friends on the dock, the steamer moved slowly out into New York harbor. A dense fog gripped the New York area and the ship was quickly swallowed up in the drifting mist.

Little Eleanor was anxious to inspect the ship and her father took her around to the various decks and to the bridge where the captain was giving orders to the helmsman. Everything seemed calm and serene as the ship glided almost silently through the fog on a glassy sea. Suddenly a foghorn sounded close abeam in the thick fog. Orders were shouted and seamen began to scurry around the decks to their assigned stations. Then out of the fog came the bow of another ship, poised like a giant knife. With a shuddering crunch the ships collided. Now gongs and whistles were sounding, and crew and passengers were ordered to abandon-ship stations. There was no time to search for belongings. Mr. Roosevelt quickly placed a life preserver on Eleanor and then took her to the side of the ship. A small lifeboat bobbed up and down on the water just below the rail, but there was no ladder to reach it. Thinking quickly, Eleanor's father gave her to a crewman and then catching a rope that dangled from an upper deck, he slid down the side and into the lifeboat. Desperately trying to maintain his balance, he then called up to the seaman to drop Eleanor.

Shrieking in terror, the little girl clung with desperation to the sailor as he lifted her over the side. It seemed such a great distance to where her father bobbed around, barely able to stand upright. At last the sailor was able to break her grasp and she felt herself tumbling through the air, screaming all the way. Then, with a gentle thump, she landed in her father's arms.

As the lifeboat pulled away from the stricken ship and rowed to a waiting rescue vessel, her father sat down and held Eleanor on his lap, trying to console the terrified little girl. The incident made a lasting impression on Eleanor Roosevelt and it was many years before she overcame her fear of the ocean.

"With my father I was perfectly happy," Eleanor recalled in later years. "He was the center of my world."

In the year 1890, when Eleanor was six years old, her father was badly injured in a riding accident. For several months he hobbled about on crutches and endured terrible pain as bones failed to heal and had to be rebroken and set again. For a man who had led such an active life, the strain of quiet convalescence seemed to break his spirit. Little Eleanor cried herself to sleep many nights as she watched her once-robust father suffer.

It was decided that a trip abroad would help Mr. Roosevelt regain his health and in the fall of that year, the family sailed to Italy for the winter. For awhile Mr. Roosevelt seemed to improve and Eleanor would always remember her delight as her father, acting as gondolier, took her along the canals of Venice in a gondola. Later they visited Naples and Mount Vesuvius before going on to Germany and then to France. In Paris, Mr. Roosevelt entered a sanitarium and Eleanor was sent to a convent to study French. It was at this time that another brother was born. He was named Hall but somehow got the nickname "Josh" that was to stay with him all his life.

A few months later, the family returned to New York from France, leaving Mr. Roosevelt to convalesce in the sanitarium. Sometime later his brother, Theodore, went to France and brought the ailing man home to America. After his arrival, he entered a rest home in Abington, Virginia.

Eleanor looked forward eagerly to the rare visits her father made to New York. These were treasured, happy moments that seemed to shine through the clouds of her rather unhappy little world. She did not want for the material things of life, of course, but she was a lonely little girl who had an unfulfilled need for genuine affection and love. Somehow, though these were always lacking in her childhood, she developed a tremendous capacity to love others.

Not long after Eleanor passed her eighth birthday, an epidemic of diphtheria swept New York. Care was taken to protect the children and Eleanor was sent to live with family friends while her brothers were sent to stay with an aunt. But Eleanor's mother was stricken. In those days there was no antitoxin for the disease and it was frequently fatal. Mr. Roosevelt rushed home from Virginia to be at his wife's bedside, but he arrived too late. Eleanor's mother was dead at the age of twenty-nine.

Death had little meaning for Eleanor at the age of eight, especially since she did not attend her mother's funeral. There was one happy fact, however, which to Eleanor *was* meaningful, and that was that her father was in New York for a visit. After the funeral, her father came to see her. Eleanor would always remember that visit.

"He was dressed all in black, looking very sad," she recalled. "He held out his arms and gathered me to him. In a little while he began to talk, to explain to me that my mother was gone, that she had been all the world to him, and now he had only my brothers and myself, that my brothers were very young and that he and I must keep close together."

Eleanor and her brothers were to live with their Grandmother Hall. When her father left to return to Virginia, "he told me to write to him often, to be a good girl, not to give any trouble, to study hard, to grow up into a woman he could be proud of, and he would come to see me whenever it was possible."

And so began a secret dreamworld for Eleanor. She dreamed that her father would recover his full health and vigor and, in a few years when she was older, that he would come for her and together they would establish a household of their own. In her dreamworld she would become a mother to her little brothers and the family would be reunited. This dream sustained Eleanor in the lonely months ahead.

Eleanor Roosevelt (right) with her brother Elliott, also known as "Ellie." She holds his hand firmly to keep him from running away from the camera.

Then tragedy struck again. Five months after the death of her mother, "Ellie," as Elliott, Jr. was called, died of diphtheria. The little world of Eleanor Roosevelt was crumbling.

Months passed—long, lonely months brightened only by an occasional visit from her father. She never knew when he was coming, but as soon as he entered the house a delighted Eleanor—a bundle of ribbons and petticoats—would fling herself into his arms. On Christmas morning in 1893, he showed up at the door with a great armload of gifts and a stocking filled with goodies.

Between visits, Eleanor and her father kept up an active correspondence. His letters were filled with tidbits of advice or questions about her animals at the estate at Tivoli. He also wrote hopefully of trips they might take together when he was well. Once or twice she wrote him a note in French just to show off the language skills she had acquired. Sometimes many weeks went by without a letter from him. Then one would arrive, full of apologies and with the explanation that he had been quite ill. One day in the summer of 1894, a telegram arrived from Abington, Virginia. Eleanor's aunts and grandmother called her into the library to tell her the terrible news—her father was dead.

"I simply refused to believe it," Eleanor remembered later, "and while I wept long and went to bed still weeping I finally went to sleep and began the next day living in my dreamworld as usual."

Now Eleanor was more lonely than ever before—a shy, rather awkward, not very pretty little orphan girl, not quite ten years old. Grandmother Hall became the guardian of Eleanor and Josh. It was certain that they would never want for material things, although Grandmother Hall insisted on keeping her granddaughter away from the things other girls of her age and social position were experiencing. But to find the deep love and affection she so badly needed, Eleanor retreated into her dreamworld where only she and her father existed. "I lived with him more closely, probably, than I had when he was alive," she wrote later.

This tragic period, and the few years which followed, were to have a marked influence on Eleanor Roosevelt. To suddenly find one's self an orphan is a traumatic experience no matter how many kind and concerned relatives try to ease the agony. Many children in the same circumstances retreat as Eleanor did into a world of make-believe. Most emerge again into the world of reality as they grow older and, with strength and courage, forge a new and happy life for themselves.

So it was to be with Eleanor Roosevelt. It would be a long and difficult battle, however, made all the more difficult by the circumstances of later years. But the tremendous need for love and the wonderful capacity to love others would sustain her throughout the most trying times. This lonely girl would one day be called the First Lady of the World.

On a summer day in 1894, Eleanor's aunts and grandmother call her into the library to tell her that her father is dead. The little girl cried herself to sleep that night, but the next day continued to live in her private dreamworld.

The Frightened Orphan

Grandmother Hall's house on Thirty-seventh Street was similar to most of the fine old brownstone houses in New York near the turn of the century. There was no electricity and the high-ceilinged rooms were rather dimly lighted by gaslights (considered almost a luxury) or candles. The servants' quarters were in the basement and the master bedrooms were on the second floor. Eleanor was given a room to herself while little Josh shared a room with the children's young Aunt Maude. Everything was done to make the orphans as comfortable as possible.

The house was a bustling place during the daytime. Besides Maude, there was also another young aunt called Pussie, two uncles—Vallie and Eddie—and the household staff. The staff con-

sisted of a laundress, a butler, a cook, and a maid. Over the whole establishment, Grandmother Hall ruled with stern discipline.

The Halls were active people who bustled about their daily lives with confidence and vigor. Uncle Eddie was not at home very much. He loved travel and adventure and frequently took trips to some far-off land, only to pop in unexpectedly months later with exciting tales of an African safari or a trip to the South Seas. His older brother, Vallie, was a dashing sportsman and businessman. A champion tennis player and horseman, he reminded Eleanor of her father in some ways.

For a long while, Eleanor was somewhat fearful of her grandmother, the stern and imposing figure who governed

A frightened Eleanor steals out to the back yard of the big house on Thirty-seventh Street to bring ice for her Aunt Pussie. Though she was terrified to go outside at night, her admiration for her aunt and her desire to be of service to others helped her overcome her fears.

the household with quiet efficiency. As time went on, however, Eleanor learned that her grandmother was never unkind and that all her decisions were made for what she considered to be the good of the family. When Grandmother Hall found that Eleanor suffered occasionally from tonsilitis or a sore throat, she prescribed a cold bath for the girl every morning during the winter. These, of course, were sheer misery for Eleanor and she would often "cheat" and add some warm water to the tub when no one was looking. She resented having to endure this ritual every morning, but later came to realize that her grandmother was convinced that it would help keep Eleanor strong and healthy. Perhaps it did, for Eleanor was never ill during the years she lived with her grandmother.

It was Aunt Pussie who most attracted Eleanor. She was young, vivacious, beautiful, talented, and artistic —all virtues which Eleanor felt she did not have now and would never have. She viewed her aunt with a mixture of envy and admiration. Though Eleanor studied the piano for several years, she never matched her Aunt Pussie's ability to play with ease and feeling. Pussie was the picture of grace and lightness when dancing, while Eleanor felt stiff and awkward. Yet she would always try to please her aunt who, in turn, encouraged the hesitant little girl.

Aunt Pussie had one outstanding shortcoming that was a source of pain and worry to Eleanor. Pussie was excessively temperamental. One moment she would be carefree and gay, and the next moment she would plunge into a mood of despair and gloom—sometimes lasting for days. At first Eleanor took Pussie's changing moods to heart, often feeling that her aunt was angry with her personally. Later she grew to understand her temperamental aunt, and during her gloomy periods Eleanor found companionship with Pussie's younger sister Maude. Watching the moody Pussie made Eleanor determined, even as a little girl, to retain her poise and self-control at all times, for she never wanted to inflict her own temporarily bad disposition on others. This trait would serve her well in later years when she would be so much in the public eye.

Eleanor's education consisted entirely of private schooling—either with tutors who taught her languages and mathematics, or in exclusive girls' schools. Besides her piano lessons, she also studied ballet and ballroom dancing. She was required to maintain a regular schedule of hours at her grandmother's house, just as if she were in a boarding school, however. Part of her training was also devoted to sewing, embroidery, hemming, and darning, and there were sessions in social etiquette.

Despite her shyness, Eleanor was a bright little girl who learned things quite easily, though she did admit having difficulty with mathematics. She especially loved literature and soon became a voracious reader. Eleanor had known French before she knew English, for she had had a French nurse. In time, she memorized many hymns and verses from the Bible in that language.

The first winter with the Hall family passed quickly for Eleanor. Each busy week was followed by a pleasant Sunday which began with the family going to church. In the afternoon there was often a walk in the park or a carriage ride through the streets of New York. There were no automobiles in those days, of course, and even the streetcars were horsedrawn. In the evening the family would gather in the library to sing hymns as Aunt Pussie played the piano. A great roaring fire in the fireplace cast flickering lights and shadows as it warmed the room.

Sunday was often the day for "good works" also, and through these, Eleanor became exposed early to people vastly different from herself. She sometimes went with her aunts or uncles to visit children's hospitals. On one occasion she and her Uncle Vallie decorated a Christmas tree for a group of underprivileged children in the infamous section of New York known as "Hell's Kitchen." These sojourns into another kind of world had a marked influence on Eleanor Roosevelt. She could see for herself the great contrast between her world of plenty and the poverty-stricken world that existed not many blocks

from her home. It was here that she first began to acquire the deep compassion for other people that was to endear her to the world.

In spite of all her training and exposure to various situations, Eleanor remained a shy and rather timid little girl, since everything she did was very structured and organized. "Looking back I see that I was always afraid of something," she remembered later, "of the dark, of displeasing people, of failure." She was rarely able to overcome these fears for herself alone. Yet she would muster her courage to be of service to other people.

Late one evening her Aunt Pussie was feeling ill and asked Eleanor to go to the icebox in the yard and bring her some ice. The house was darkened, for everyone else was in bed, which meant that Eleanor would have to make a terrifying trip down the stairs and through the pitch-black basement to reach the yard and the icebox. If it had been for herself, she would have done without the ice rather than venture into the yard at night. But because her beloved Aunt Pussie was ill, Eleanor fought off the terror that gripped her and brought the ice. The desire and need to be of service to others helped Eleanor overcome many fears and uncertainties during the years that followed.

With the coming of spring, the Hall family moved out of the city to the handsome estate called Oak Terrace

near Tivoli-on-the-Hudson. Here Eleanor had her own pony, named Captain, given to her by her father. She loved riding but later admitted that in these early years she had been too timid to make Captain go where she wanted him to go. Instead, she got on the pony's back and rode wherever he chose to go. There were also dogs and cats and other animals on the estate. Sometimes, with her dog Mickey trailing at their heels, she would ride Captain out to a shady place overlooking the river and then lie under a tree and read a book for hours at a time. She was often happiest when she was by herself. Realizing this, her grandmother had a little house built for her in some nearby woods. Here Eleanor could retreat with her books and her dreams.

There were no children her own age to play with at Tivoli, and there were periods during the summer when the aunts and uncles and Eleanor's grandmother were on vacation at Newport, Rhode Island, or in Maine. Eleanor and her brother were left in the care of the servants. She was always popular with the household staff and liked to help them with their work. The butler would let her wash and dry the dishes and she also scampered busily around the house helping the chambermaid make the beds. In return, on one or two occasions when Eleanor was punished by being sent to bed without dinner, the servants would smuggle food to the little girl.

At Tivoli, Eleanor most enjoyed helping the cheerful old German woman named Mrs. Overhalse, who did the Roosevelts' washing. There were no automatic washers in those days, of course, so Mrs. Overhalse scrubbed everything by hand. Eleanor considered it an honor and privilege to be allowed to scrub away on the washboard, or to iron napkins and towels with the irons that were heated on the stove. Their different stations in life meant nothing to the little girl who, even then, recognized that the goodness in a person does not depend upon his wealth or position.

Eleanor with her pony, Captain, who was given to her as a gift by her father. Eleanor usually let the pony go where he wanted, for she was often too afraid to make him go in a specific direction.

31

Occasionally Eleanor and her Aunt Maude would hitch Captain to a little two-wheeled cart and take rides along the country roads. One day they heard an unfamiliar sound approaching and, before they could decide what it was, around the corner chugged the first automobile either had ever seen! Captain, of course, had never seen one either, and as this strange vehicle drew nearer, the pony bolted wildly in a mad dash of terror. Cart and riders crashed headlong into a barbed wire fence, and Eleanor was thrown to the ground. No one was seriously injured, but both would always remember their first encounter with a motorcar.

As summer waned and the first cold snap of autumn crackled out of the north, the Hall family closed up the estate at Tivoli and returned to the city. For the next five years, Eleanor spent half the year in New York City and half of it at Tivoli.

In the meantime, as she became a teen-ager she was growing taller and, in fact, was growing much faster than other girls her age. Being tall can have many advantages for a girl who has the confidence and poise to make the most of her height. But poor Eleanor was still painfully shy. She would much rather have been lost in the crowd, but her height, of course, made her stand out.

To make things worse, Grandmother Hall insisted on dressing Eleanor in clothes befitting her age rather than her size. Women's styles during the years at the end of the last century called for hemlines which trailed along the ground for older women, halfway between ankles and knees for young women, and knee-length for young girls. Her grandmother dressed Eleanor in skirts that came above her knees which, of course, set her quite apart from other girls her size at parties and social events.

If this were not painful enough to endure, Eleanor was also required to wear high-buttoned shoes because she was suspected of having weak ankles. All this only emphasized her legginess and gave her a rather ungainly appearance. Eleanor's grandmother also insisted that she wear flannel underclothes from her ankles to her neck throughout the winter. This necessitated wearing long black stockings and bulky petticoats. The total effect was to dampen the spirit and increase the uncertainty that continued to plague the self-conscious girl.

In February of 1898, the battleship U.S.S. *Maine* was blown up in the harbor at Havana, Cuba. A rebellion was in progress at the time against long-time Spanish rule. War fever swept the United States and in April, the United States declared war against Spain. Eleanor's Uncle Theodore Roosevelt resigned as assistant secretary of the navy and, with Colonel Leonard Wood, formed the United States First Volunteer Cavalry Regiment. In May, Commodore George Dewey destroyed the Spanish fleet at Manila Bay in the Philippines, and in June the army landed in Cuba. The Hall family had always tried to keep Eleanor and her brother away from the influence of their Roosevelt relatives. They did not concern themselves too much with political and international news, but Eleanor often saw her uncle's name mentioned in the newspapers. In July, 1898, she found his name in the headlines of every paper. Theodore Roosevelt had led the

The sight and sound of an automobile frightens the pony, Captain. He is pulling a cart carrying Eleanor and her Aunt Maude on an afternoon jaunt. The pony proceeds to drag the cart into a barbed wire fence, but fortunately neither occupant of the cart was injured.

charge of the "Rough Riders," his cavalry regiment, up San Juan Hill. He was the hero of the day. Later in the year when the war was over, he returned home and was elected governor of New York.

Once each summer, and again at Christmastime, Eleanor was invited to spend a few days with her Uncle Ted at his Sagamore Hill home in Oyster Bay on Long Island. This was one of the few times during the year that Eleanor saw her father's family. She always enjoyed these holidays with the robust Roosevelt clan, although she rather dreaded having to participate in the athletic games that her uncle organized. To cap the holiday, Uncle Ted usually gave a dance for all the children. Ordinarily, Eleanor hated this part of the vacation, for seldom was she noticed by the other guests. It was at one of these parties, in 1898, that a significant event occurred in Eleanor's life. She was sitting in torment and mortification watching the others dance and hoping that no one would notice her "different" dress. Suddenly, she became aware of a handsome young man standing beside her with a bright and friendly smile.

"Would you care to dance?" he asked.

She managed a breathless "Yes" and Franklin Roosevelt, her distant cousin, extended his arm and led her smilingly to the dance floor. They had met only once before—when she was two and he was four—but she had heard occasionally of this bright young man from Hyde Park.

Once on the dance floor, her shyness disappeared in the face of Franklin's amiable personality. Soon they were talking with ease on many subjects. They were attracted to one another from the very first, though saying it was "love at first sight" is perhaps too exaggerated. At this time, Eleanor was fourteen and Franklin was sixteen. The handsome youth discovered the inner beauty of the shy, plain girl. The broad smile that seemed to encompass her whole face reflected the many virtues that lay concealed behind the too-short dress. The spectators saw only two young people dancing together, and that this youthful pair were destined to make world history could never have been suspected.

After five years of living in her grandmother's household, Eleanor was sent off to England to be educated. This had always been one of Eleanor's mother's fondest hopes for her daughter, and Grandmother Hall decided that the time had come. Soon after her fifteenth birthday, in the autumn of 1899, Eleanor sailed for England with her Aunt Tissie Mortimer, who was Pussie's and Maude's married older sister.

The voyage marked a turning point in Eleanor Roosevelt's life. For the first time she was to be away from family control and on her own to a large extent. In the coming years, she would lose her childhood fears and gain a large measure of self-confidence. She would owe this change mainly to the person who waited to greet her at the end of the voyage.

At a party given by her Uncle Theodore, Eleanor dances with her handsome fifth cousin Franklin Roosevelt.

Travels with Mlle. Souvestre

Mademoiselle Souvestre was the headmistress of the Allenswood School near London which Eleanor would attend for the next three years. Aunt Tissie delivered Eleanor to Mlle. Souvestre and then hastened off to London with the promise that they would share Christmas together. At first, Eleanor was quite lonely, but Mlle. Souvestre quickly made her feel welcome. When Eleanor had unpacked her belongings, the headmistress invited her to the library for a chat to get better acquainted.

"Mlle. Souvestre was short and rather stout," Eleanor remembered later, "she had snow-white hair. Her head was beautiful, with clear-cut, strong features, a strong face and a broad forehead. Her hair grew to a peak in front and waved back in natural waves to a twist at the back of her head. Her eyes looked through you, and she always knew more than she was told.

"Mlle. Souvestre . . . had a soft spot for Americans and liked them as pupils," Eleanor continued. "From the start Mlle. Souvestre was interested in me . . . and day by day I found myself more interested in her."

The warm bond of friendship which quickly formed between the old lady and the teen-ager made life much more pleasant for Eleanor. She had looked forward to an easier way of life in England, but there was an even more rigid set of rules at Allenswood than there had been in her grandmother's house. Here, however, the rules were designed not for her alone, but for the entire student body. She found that the five years with her grandmother had prepared her well for the school regime, and she adapted very quickly.

The first and foremost rule which had to be obeyed at Allenswood was that everyone must speak only French. This, of course, presented no real problem to Eleanor, since she had learned French even before she learned English and had been speaking French almost daily ever since. All the classes were taught in French except Shakespeare and, of course, languages such as Latin or German.

The daily routine at Allenswood began early. The girls had to make their beds neatly before leaving the room for the continental breakfast, or *petit*

Eleanor takes an exciting train ride through the Alps. She was traveling to meet her Uncle Henry and Aunt Tissie Mortimer at Saint Moritz in Switzerland, to spend the summer with them.

déjeuner. This consisted of café au lait (coffee with milk) and rolls with butter and jam. Breakfast was followed year-round by a brisk walk in a nearby park. English winter weather is not for the fainthearted; but, come drizzle, rain, or dripping fog, girls were rarely excused from this daily exercise. Eleanor had looked forward to shedding the hated flannel undergarments which her grandmother had insisted she wear. After two or three morning excursions in the chilling English dampness, however, she began wearing them again. The British keep their homes and buildings at a much lower temperature than do Americans, and Eleanor found that she was perfectly comfortable in her flannels, indoors or out.

Every hour of the day was scheduled and accounted for. Certain hours were for music practice or for study. Other hours were set aside for athletics. For the first time, Eleanor overcame her awkwardness and became a star at field hockey. Once a week time was set aside for sewing, mending, and darning, since each girl was expected to care for her own wardrobe. A few girls who were favorites of Mlle. Souvestre were invited on certain evenings to join her in the study. There the headmistress would read poetry aloud, or stories and plays. Eleanor was delighted to be accorded this honor and pleased her teacher with recitations of her own.

In her new surroundings, Eleanor began to emerge from the shell she had built around herself for so many years. ". . . I felt I was starting a new life," she said, "free from all my former sins. This was the first time in my life that my fears left me. If I lived up to the rules and told the truth, there was nothing to fear." For the first time, too, a new trait began to take shape in Eleanor Roosevelt—that of self-confidence.

Eleanor made several close and lasting friendships while at the Allenswood School. There was Carola de Passavant from Germany; Avice Horn from Australia; Marjorie Bennett, an English girl who was Eleanor's roommate; and Helen Gifford, who later grew up to become headmistress of a school similar to Allenswood. Perhaps her closest friend of the period was Hilda "Burky" Burkinshaw, an English girl whose family lived in India. Most of these friendships lasted for many years. Eleanor, in fact, was one day to become godmother to Burky's daughter.

By the time the Christmas holidays rolled around, Eleanor was very much at home in England. She journeyed by herself to London for Christmas dinner at Claridge's Hotel with Aunt Tissie and her family. Then she traveled to the north of England to spend a few days with some English relatives before going to Paris to bid good-bye to Aunt Tissie, who was just leaving for Switzerland. In later years, Eleanor would look back and "marvel at my confidence and independence, for I was totally without fear in this new phase of my life."

Back at Allenswood School, Eleanor renewed her education. At this time England was engaged in the Boer War in South Africa. Eleanor often read the exciting accounts of the fighting which were written by a youthful newspaper correspondent named Winston Churchill. Mlle. Souvestre could not accept the British position in the war and openly expressed sentiments in favor of the Boers. Of course, most of her girls were English and she understood their point of view. She allowed celebrations after an English victory, but she would not participate. Eleanor admired Mlle. Souvestre's theories about the rights of smaller nations to govern themselves, and also her tolerance for the views of others.

When summer vacation rolled around, Eleanor was in a tizzy of excitement. She had been invited to spend the summer with her aunt and uncle, the Mortimers, at Saint Moritz in Switzerland. Riding on the train, she was filled with wonder at the sight of the snow-capped majesty of the Swiss Alps and the quaint chalets perched on the mountainsides. Their hotel overlooked the lake with the towering Alps as its backdrop, and Eleanor decided that these mountains were even more beautiful than the Catskills of her native New York. To top off the season, Eleanor, her aunt, and a friend traveled by carriage across the Austrian Tyrol to Oberammergau, Germany, to see the world-renowned Passion Play. This play is staged only every ten years, and all of the townspeople of Oberammergau take part in it. In the audience that year was a youthful college principal who, like Eleanor Roosevelt, was destined to world fame as a humanitarian. His name was Albert Schweitzer.

The summer vacation too quickly over, Eleanor returned to Allenswood and her studies with Mlle. Souvestre. The headmistress listened with interest to Eleanor's breathless tales of her summer travels and told the girl that perhaps the two of them could travel together someday. Eleanor, of course, was delighted at this suggestion.

On January 22, 1901, Queen Victoria died after sixty-four years on England's throne, the longest reign in that country's history. The British Isles, indeed the whole world, was plunged into mourning. Eleanor went to London to view the funeral procession, and it made a profound impression on the girl from New York.

"I have never forgotten," she wrote years later, "the great emotional force that seemed to stir all about us as Queen Victoria, so small in stature and yet so great in devotion to her people, passed out of their lives forever."

At Easter vacation, Mlle. Souvestre took Eleanor on a tour of southern Europe. They began by traveling leisurely to Marseilles, where they spent a day or two, then catching a train for Pisa. All her young life, Eleanor had been trained to plan things with meticulous care and to follow precisely the schedule laid out. Nothing had ever been done on the spur of the moment. But Mlle. Souvestre did not like to travel that way. On the way to Pisa, as the train slowed for a scheduled stop, Mlle. Souvestre suddenly jumped up and said, "This is Alassio. I have a friend here. Let's get off!" Stunned and surprised, Eleanor hastily gathered the light baggage and they dismounted from the train, which pulled out with all their heavy bags in the baggage car. As it turned out, the friend was not at home, so Eleanor and her somewhat unpredictable companion spent a lovely hour walking along the beach. Then they caught the next train to Pisa.

"I had learned a valuable lesson," Eleanor decided. "Never again would I be the rigid little person I had been theretofore."

Throughout the trip, Mlle. Souvestre gave Eleanor the responsibility of packing and unpacking the luggage and checking train schedules, buying tickets, and arranging other transportation. For the first time in her life, Eleanor was given some real responsibility and with her new-found confidence, she came through with flying colors.

Her confidence was given another big boost during their stay in Florence, that famous city of art treasures in northern Italy. Mlle. Souvestre felt that walking around the streets would be too tiring for her. " . . . but the only way to know a city really is to walk its streets," she told Eleanor. "Florence is worth it. . . . go and see it."

And so, against all her previous training, Eleanor went—unescorted and unchaperoned—to walk the streets of a strange foreign city. Her grandmother would have been horrified had she known. But Eleanor found everyone most kind and helpful, showing her the way when she was lost, advising her where to eat, and suggesting where to shop for the best bargains. Unlike many tourists, Eleanor ate Italian foods, sipped Italian wine (for the water was bad), and chatted in French or Italian with the local populace. Mlle. Souvestre had told her that to see a foreign country, one had to mingle with the people; Eleanor found that this was very true.

The days passed swiftly, and soon the travelers hastened back to England to resume their school duties. With her

Mlle. Souvestre took Eleanor and Burky to Rome. Here they are shown viewing the Colosseum.

meager allowance, Eleanor had just been able to purchase gifts for everyone back in New York. She looked forward to returning home to deliver them in person. When summer came, she bid good-bye to the Allenswood School and sailed home with Aunt Pussie, who had been visiting the Mortimers. She promised to be back for the reopening of school in the autumn.

The summer was quite boring for Eleanor. She spent most of her time with relatives in New England, but after two years in England and Europe, she had little in common with the younger people of the area. She was anxious to return to the Old World and the many warm friends she had met there. At last her grandmother said she could go for another year, providing she could find a suitable traveling companion to accompany her on the ship. Since none of the relatives or family friends were going to Europe, Eleanor hired a woman to accompany her. This satisfied Grandmother Hall's concern that she be chaperoned, even though none of the family met the companion before the trip began. It turned out that Eleanor was a far more experienced traveler than was her companion and she never saw the woman from the time they boarded the ship until they arrived in England.

Eleanor took up her studies once again, delighted to be back with her school friends and her beloved Mlle. Souvestre. Soon after her arrival in England, she learned that President William McKinley had been shot at the Pan American Exposition in Buffalo, New York. Theodore Roosevelt, who was now the vice-president, hastened to Washington to guide the nation until the President recovered from his wounds. President McKinley, however, died a week later on September 14, 1901—the third president in our history to be assassinated. Eleanor's Uncle Ted now became the twenty-sixth president of the United States.

For the Christmas holidays that year, the headmistress took Eleanor and her friend Burky to Rome. There they visited the Colosseum and the Forum as Mlle. Souvestre related the historic significance of each. They also visited the famed Tivoli Gardens and St. Peter's Cathedral. As usual, Eleanor was thoroughly delighted with the trip, and it was made all the more meaningful and exciting by the presence of Mlle. Souvestre.

For the Easter holidays of 1902, the gracious headmistress invited Eleanor to accompany her on a visit to friends in northern France and Belgium. Then they journeyed up the Rhine to Frankfort for a visit with the family of Carola de Passavant, one of Eleanor's classmates. At last the time came to return to school.

Summer arrived and Eleanor prepared to return to America. She was sorry to leave, but with youthful optimism she hoped to come back again to travel with her elderly friend. "I realize now that Mlle. Souvestre, knowing her infirmities, had little hope of seeing me again," Eleanor recalled in later years. "She wrote me lovely letters, which I still cherish. They show the kind of relationship that had grown up between us and give an idea of the fine person who exerted the greatest influence, after my father, on this period of my life."

And so, in the summer of 1902, Eleanor Roosevelt returned home for good. No longer was she the fearful, uncertain little girl who had sailed to England three years before. Due to the kindness and training of her dear friend Mlle. Souvestre, she was now a confident young lady—well traveled, well read, and well educated. She would never see Mlle. Souvestre again but the affectionate memory of this lovely lady, and a debt of gratitude to her, would remain with Eleanor Roosevelt all the years of her life.

From Miss to Mrs. Roosevelt

By the time Eleanor arrived home in the summer of 1902, Grandmother Hall had moved back to the country estate at Tivoli. Here Eleanor spent the whole summer and in the early autumn moved to the big house in New York City with her Aunt Pussie. There was no more thought of school for Eleanor, for Grandmother Hall attached great importance to "coming out" as a debutante at the age of eighteen. Eleanor had now reached her eighteenth birthday and so must be formally introduced to New York society.

Eleanor's name was placed on the lists of family friends and relatives for invitations to the many parties and balls given that winter. After three years of a rather informal way of life in Europe, Eleanor was hesitant at first to accept any invitations. At last she felt she must, however, and went to an Assembly Ball with her cousins Mr. and Mrs. Henry Parish. For Eleanor it was quite a disappointment.

"I imagine that I was well dressed," she would recall in later years, "but there was absolutely nothing about me to attract anybody's attention. . . . I do not think I quite realized beforehand what utter agony it was going to be or I would never have had the courage to go. . . . by no stretch of the imagination could I fool myself into thinking that I was a popular debutante! I went home early, thankful to get away. . . . I knew I was the first girl in my mother's family who was not a belle and, though I never acknowledged it to any of them at the time, I was deeply ashamed."

Eleanor was expected to give parties of her own, and she and Pussie (who was still unmarried) gave several luncheons and occasionally a dinner. Aunt Tissie Mortimer, with whom Eleanor had attended the Passion Play at Oberammergau, gave a large party in Eleanor's honor, too—a supper and theater performance followed by dancing. Eleanor grew to know most of the

Eleanor Roosevelt as a debutante in 1902. Her Grandmother Hall insisted that she "come out" as a debutante at the age of eighteen, though Eleanor would have preferred not to join the social whirl of New York's high society.

Eleanor's work on the Junior League took her into the slums of New York City, to work with the children who lived there.

people of the high-society set before the winter was over.

Eleanor was eager to be a social success and to become a part of the social whirl as was expected of her. As the weeks and months passed, however, she grew tired of the formality and the never-ending round of balls and dinner parties. She began to seek out less formal groups. An old friend by the name of Bob Ferguson introduced her to several painters and musicians. Her artistic Aunt Pussie often took her to the theater, concerts, or the opera where Eleanor made many other informal acquaintances. Little by little Eleanor came to decide that New York society was not really as important as she had believed.

As her interest in formal affairs of high society began to fade, Eleanor searched for new interests. Her natural instinct for service to others led her to join the Junior League, just then being formed among a few other like-minded society members. Now she spent much of her time working with children in the slum areas of New York City. Later she joined the Consumers League, which conducted investigations into the working conditions of women employed in the garment industry. This particular industry was notorious for many years for its almost indescribably bad working conditions and virtual slave labor. The Consumers League also looked into the conditions for women workers in department stores. Eleanor usually went on these "inspection tours" with women who had more experience in these matters, but she still had to muster her courage and determination in the face of harried and often irate foremen and store managers.

The months passed quickly, and in 1903 romance entered the life of Eleanor Roosevelt. Her fifth cousin Franklin had been seeing her quite often between semesters at Harvard. They seemed to have many interests in common and their friendship soon turned to love.

The formalities of boy-girl relationships in those days makes one wonder how two people could ever get to know each other, let alone fall in love. Eleanor described some of these formalities in her autobiography.

"It was understood that no girl was interested in a man or showed any liking for him until he had made all the advances. You knew a man very well before you wrote or received a letter from him, and those letters make me smile when I see some of the correspondence today." Letters to Eleanor always began "Dear Miss Roosevelt" and were signed "Very sincerely yours." To have signed them any other way would have been a "breach of good manners," Eleanor reported.

"You never allowed a man to give you a present except flowers or candy or possibly a book," she said, " . . . and the idea that you would permit any man to kiss you before you were engaged to him never even crossed my mind."

Despite all this, Franklin and Eleanor fell in love and, in the fall of 1903, he asked her to marry him. She quickly accepted his proposal, but his widowed mother did not readily approve. She immediately took Franklin out of school and whisked him off to the West Indies for the winter, hoping his feelings would change. They did not, however, and in the autumn of 1904 Franklin and Eleanor's engagement was announced.

From the time of Franklin's proposal until their marriage, the young couple spent much time together—always chaperoned, of course, by a maid or members of the family. The Delanos, Franklin's mother's family, were a happy, robust lot descended from seafarers of old New England. In the summer of 1904, Eleanor was invited to join in their traditional reunion at the family home in Fairhaven, Massachusetts.

". . . this first big family party at Fairhaven was to me something of a revelation," wrote the orphan girl who had never really known her own family. "There was a sense of security which I had never known before. . . . The Delanos were the first people I met who were able to do what they wanted to do without wondering where to obtain the money, and it was not long before I learned the reason for this. . . . They watched their pennies, which I had always seen squandered. They were generous and could afford to be in big things, because so little was ever wasted or spent in inconsequential ways."

The Delano family was also loyal. "If misfortune befell one of them, the others rallied at once. . . . The Delanos might disapprove of one another, and if so they were not slow to express their disapproval, but let someone outside so much as hint at criticism and the clan was ready to tear him limb from limb!"

Eleanor enjoys herself at the Delano family reunion in the summer of 1904. The Delanos accepted her as one of their own, and she marveled at the loyalty and security this family felt.

Eleanor was accepted at once as a member of the clan, and she was thankful for the sense of security and belonging that the Delano family inspired even before she and Franklin were actually married.

The wedding was set for St. Patrick's Day, March 17, 1905. In the meantime, Franklin had graduated from Harvard and entered law school at Columbia University in New York. His mother took a house in the city to be near her son. The young couple went through a round of parties during those hectic months before the marriage. Eleanor was assisted by her cousin, Mrs. Henry Parish, in selecting her trousseau, and wedding gifts began to arrive from friends and relatives all over the world.

On March 4, 1905, just two weeks before the wedding, Eleanor's Uncle Ted was inaugurated as president, having been re-elected the previous November. Eleanor and Franklin attended the ceremonies at the Capitol in Washington, D.C. After the inauguration, they were invited to the White House for lunch and watched the inaugural parade. "I told myself I had seen a historical event," Eleanor wrote later, "and I never expected to see another inauguration in the family!" Of course she was to see many more, for the handsome young man who held her hand on the train ride back to New York was inaugurated four consecutive times, thirty years later.

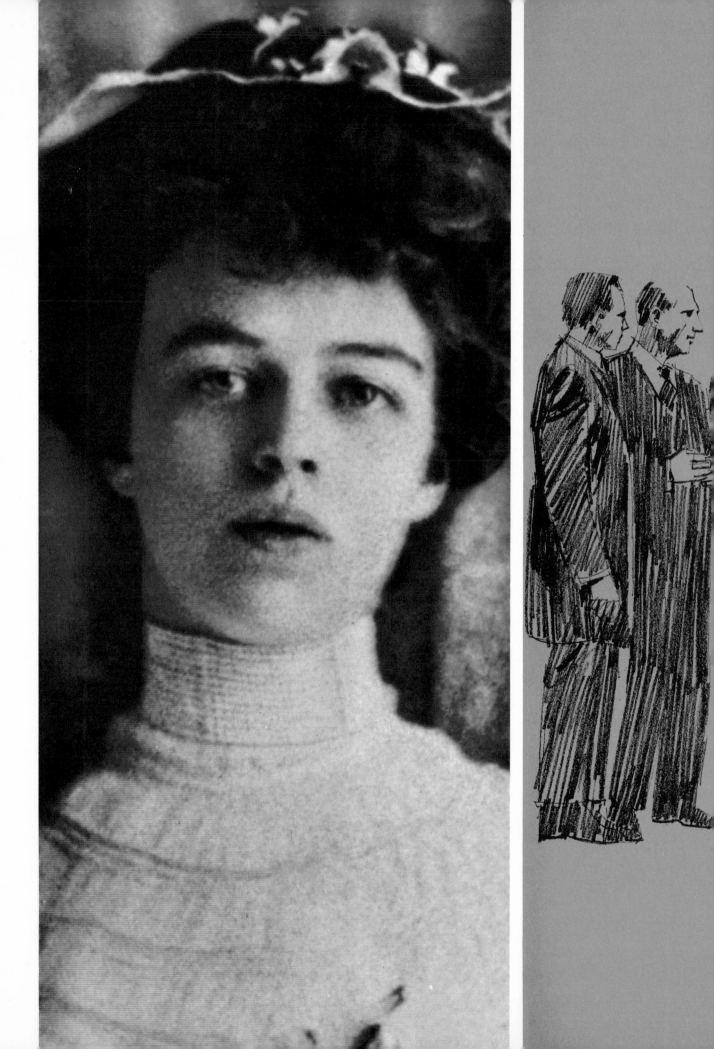

Left, a portrait of Eleanor as a bride, on March 17, 1905. Above, the guests at Eleanor and Franklin's wedding gather around Uncle Ted as he tells some of his famous stories in the library.

The next two weeks were a frenzied blur of excitement for all those actively involved in the wedding preparations. Like most brides-to-be, Eleanor was in a whirl from morning till night. Some of Eleanor's bridesmaids offered to help her write thank-you notes for the wedding gifts. This, too, caused a panic that Eleanor could look back upon with a smile in later years. "One day we discovered to our horror that Isabelle Selmes was writing 'Franklin and I are so pleased with your gift,' etc. and then signing her own name instead of mine!"

At last the big day arrived and Uncle Ted took time out to come to New York to give away the bride and to participate in New York's St. Patrick's Day parade. The ceremony was held at the home of her cousin, Susie Parish. Of course the crowds were enormous due to the presence of the President. The singing of "The Wearin' o' the Green" in the streets outside nearly drowned out the services inside the house. Otherwise, the beautiful affair went off without a hitch. Miss Roosevelt became Mrs. Roosevelt.

The bride was lovely in a dress of "heavy stiff satin, with shirred tulle in the neck, and long sleeves. My Grandmother Hall's rose-point Brussels lace covered the dress, and a veil of the same lace fell from my head over my long train." Eleanor also wore a "dog-collar" of pearls given to her by her mother-in-law, and carried a large bouquet of lilies of the valley.

After the ceremony, the bride and groom were surrounded by well-wishers, but suddenly the crowd began to thin and soon they were virtually alone. The President, it seemed, had moved into the library and was telling one of his famous stories, and the crowd had followed to listen. Eleanor was used to this—she knew her Uncle Ted. With a shrug and a grin she said, "Well, let's go join the crowd!" And so the newlyweds meandered hand in hand into the library and stood at the back of the crowd. At last Uncle Ted had to leave for Washington and the crowd turned its interest once more to the young couple. Later the young Mr. and Mrs. Roosevelt left in a shower of rice for a brief honeymoon at Franklin's family home at Hyde Park. It was a short holiday because Franklin had to return to his law studies at Columbia.

The newlyweds began housekeeping in a small apartment not far from the university. Eleanor's younger brother, Hall, moved in with the couple during the Easter holiday. They had a housekeeper, so there was really little for Eleanor to do except the sewing and mending. When Franklin finished his term at Columbia Law School in the summer of 1905, the couple took their "second honeymoon." Now they had the time for a truly wonderful trip to London and Paris, then on to Milan and Venice in Italy, and then Germany. Later they visited Scotland where their newly married friends, Bob Ferguson and Isabelle Selmes, were honeymooning.

One day Eleanor was somewhat embarrassed when a Scottish woman asked her to explain the difference between American state and national governments. Eleanor had never been encouraged to be interested in government or politics, and could not answer the lady's question. However, she made "a vow that once safely back in the United States I would find out something about my own government." This was the beginning of a growing awareness and interest in various forms of government. Eleanor had many opportunities to learn during the years ahead.

After the second honeymoon was over, Franklin and Eleanor moved into a house in New York which Franklin's mother had rented for them. She had also furnished and decorated the house and had hired the household staff. It was a most generous gesture, but it also marked the beginning of many years of domination by Eleanor's mother-in-law. Later, Mrs. Roosevelt had a home built for Eleanor and Franklin right next to hers on East Sixty-fifth Street. The house had connecting doors, which placed Eleanor even more under her mother-in-law's control.

For the first few years of married life, Eleanor "was always just getting over having a baby or about to have one." Their first child, Anna, was born in May of 1906 and James was born in December of 1907. A third child, born in March of 1909, died of influenza eight months later. Then, in September, 1910, another boy was born and named Elliott, for Eleanor's father.

Meanwhile, Eleanor was rapidly losing the ability to think for herself, which she had gained while in school in England. Her mother-in-law had convinced her to give up her social service work because she might bring home diseases from the slums. Since her mother-in-law ran the household, there was little for Eleanor to do at home. She knew nothing of cooking and other household chores and little or nothing about child care, which she left mostly to the nurses. She wanted to learn how to be a good housekeeper and mother, but with the household being run so efficiently by her mother-in-law, she had little opportunity to gain practical experience.

The thing Eleanor began to long for most was a home of her own. She wanted a house she could furnish to her taste, staff with whatever servants she felt were necessary, and supervise on her own—even if it meant making a few mistakes while learning. Her wish came true as the year 1910 ended. At the same time, Eleanor Roosevelt began a new and important phase of her life.

Eleanor and Franklin in London on their second honeymoon. Their first honeymoon was spent at Hyde Park and was very brief, since Franklin had to go back to law school at Columbia University.

Crisis at Campobello

About the time Elliott was born, Franklin decided to try his hand in the political arena. Since his graduation from Columbia Law School, he had been associated with the law firm of Carter, Ledyard and Milburn in New York City. Uncle Ted's career had been an inspiration to the young man from Hyde Park, and the President had always encouraged young men to be of public service. When the Democratic nomination for state senator from his district was offered, Franklin could not resist. He waged a hard campaign, carrying his message directly to the people, and won—to become the first Democratic state senator from that district in thirty-two years.

Soon after the beginning of the year 1911, the Roosevelts moved to Albany, New York's capital city on the Hudson River. Here, Eleanor's wish came true. For the very first time, she was on her own and had the opportunity to furnish and manage a home to her own taste. Another aspect of this new life was the fact that Eleanor became involved in politics. She had always felt that it was a woman's duty to share her husband's life and take an active interest in his work. She began to do this immediately, though at first it was often difficult for her. It marked the beginning of her preparation for the important role she was to play in national and world affairs many years later.

Eleanor Roosevelt during the early years of her marriage. At this time she was dominated a great deal by her mother-in-law, and she ached to have a household of her very own.

The natural leadership qualities of Franklin Roosevelt were apparent right from the beginning, and he led the fight against the Tammany Hall political machine, which was the ruling power in New York City government. Eleanor's home served as a meeting place for Franklin's supporters, and she saw to it that the men were fed and made comfortable. She soon became absorbed in their struggle, and though she had no active part to play in Franklin's role as state senator, she began to learn something of the inner workings of the American political system.

Franklin ran for re-election in 1912 against Tammany Hall opposition, but before his campaign really got going, he was struck down with typhoid fever. Many feared that because of his illness, Franklin would almost certainly lose the election, for he would be unable to campaign. A former newspaperman by the name of Louis Howe, however, took over the reins of the campaign while Eleanor nursed Franklin back to health. Eleanor did not like the rather dwarfish little man who clouded up her rooms with smoke from the cigarettes which he smoked one after another. But Louis Howe, even in this early year, recognized the potentialities of Franklin Roosevelt and believed completely in a great future for the man from Hyde Park. Howe worked hard, and Franklin managed to win a second term as state senator.

Theodore Roosevelt, who had been a Republican president, did not run for re-election in 1908. He became so dissatisfied with the new Republican presi-dent, William H. Taft, however, that in 1912 he formed a third party called the Progressive, or "Bull Moose," Party. This split the Republican ranks and made it easy for Woodrow Wilson, the Democratic candidate, to win the presidential election of 1912. Franklin Roosevelt was already recognized as a brilliant young man in the Democratic ranks, and early in 1913 President Wilson appointed him assistant secretary of the navy. Eleanor now packed up the family and she, Franklin, and the three children moved to Washington, D.C.

Eleanor found that the social whirl in the nation's capital was much different from the one with which she had grown up in New York. There were seemingly endless rounds of social calls to be made on the wives of other government officials and, of course, Eleanor was expected to reciprocate with social functions of her own. Besides her own social activities, she also accompanied Franklin on official trips to various naval installations all around the country. She had hoped to broaden even further her understanding of politics and government while in Washington, and tried to do this whenever she could find the time.

Much of Eleanor's life was centered upon her family, however, and two more children were born during these years in Washington. In August of 1914, the month that World War I began in Europe, Franklin Delano Roosevelt, Jr., was born and a year and a half later, in March of 1916, John, the Roosevelts' sixth and last baby arrived. When the flu epidemic struck Washington, Eleanor really had her hands full. All of the children were sick, one with double pneumonia, and so were Franklin and three of the servants. Only Eleanor and the cook were not confined to bed, and for days they labored almost around the clock to nurse the stricken family back to health.

In April of 1917, America declared war against Germany and her allies. The pace of life quickened in America—especially in Washington, D.C. President Wilson had been preparing for war in case it became necessary to enter the rapidly expanding European conflict, but now his administration had to work overtime. During this period, Franklin had very little time at home with his family. Often he would bring associates home for lunch or dinner and Eleanor had to make careful security arrangements. Many topics were discussed which were meant to be heard only by those at the table. Eleanor worked out an arrangement whereby the servants would enter the room only when she rang a little bell which was always next to her place at the table. In this way she could eliminate the risk of secret information being heard by unauthorized persons.

Eleanor's life became very hectic during the war. Social activities were quickly forgotten, as all her spare time was devoted to supporting the war effort. Several days each week were devoted to work in the kitchen of a Red Cross canteen, preparing food for transient servicemen. She supervised the knitting of sweaters and woolen hats for soldiers. There were numerous visits to military hospitals where she passed out cigarettes and other gifts to sick and wounded servicemen. She also visited St. Elizabeth's Hospital for the mentally ill where shell-shocked veterans were sent. Here she discovered for the first time in her life how she personally could take action to improve a government institution. Conditions at St. Elizabeth's were in an extremely poor state, and Eleanor wrote a personal note to the government official responsible. She was pleased to see quick action taken to better equip the hospital to care for its patients.

When the war ended with the Armistice in November of 1918, Franklin was sent to France on official navy business. Eleanor decided to go along. Leaving the children in the care of her mother-in-law, she and Franklin sailed soon after the new year of 1919 began.

In war-torn France, Eleanor visited hospitals and toured the areas that had recently been battlefields. President and Mrs. Wilson were also in France at this time to attend the Paris peace talks. Franklin and Eleanor joined the presidential party for the trip home on the *George Washington*. The Wilsons asked the Roosevelts to lunch with them one day and much of the discussion was devoted to the League of Nations, then in its infancy. "What hopes we had that this League would really prove the instrument for the prevention of future wars," Eleanor remembered.

America was not destined to join the League of Nations, however, despite President Wilson's vigorous efforts, for

The vice-presidential campaign in 1920. Left, Eleanor and Franklin pose for a portrait. Above, the Roosevelts waving from the back of a train on a "whistle-stop" tour during the 1920 campaign.

the Senate refused to ratify the treaty making the United States a member of the organization. Consequently, the League was never very effective, as events of later years were to prove. Many idealists, including Franklin and Eleanor Roosevelt, continued to dream of such an organization, but it would take another world war to make the various nations see why a world alliance of nations was necessary. The United Nations Organization, formed at the end of World War II, offered the world a second chance. Despite its deficiencies, it was one hope for a peaceful world.

With the war over and conditions returning to normal, the Roosevelts were able to take a much-needed rest. Now they had more time to devote to their children and to happy times at the summer home on Campobello Island, New Brunswick. This little Canadian retreat, just off the coast of Maine, is a delightful spot. Here the Roosevelts could relax, swimming or deep-sea fishing off Franklin's sailboat, *Vireo*. Most of each summer was spent on the island.

It was at Campobello that, in June of 1920, Eleanor received a telegram saying that Franklin had been unanimously nominated for the vice-presidency by the National Democratic Convention being held in San Francisco. Eleanor was pleased and proud at the news of course, but was not very excited for, as she said, "I had come to accept the fact that public service was my husband's great interest and I always tried to make the necessary family adjustments easy."

In September, the presidential campaign began in earnest. Eleanor, after placing the older children safely in school and leaving the others with her mother-in-law, joined Franklin on a whistle-stop tour of the country.

When the train stopped at various small towns, she stood on the rear platform with her husband and waved to the well-wishers, listened to Franklin's speech, and shook thousands of hands. This was her first active participation in a political campaign and it took great courage to push aside her fears and face the crowds. At the larger towns and

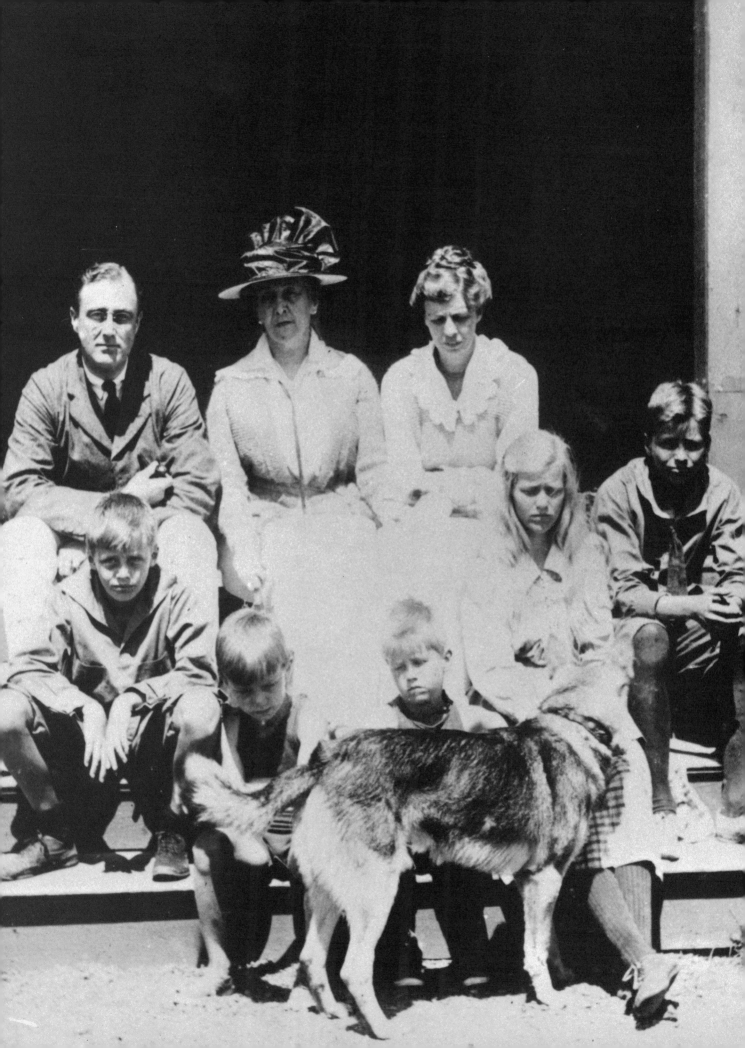

cities where Democratic rallies were held, she met the various local politicians or state government officials and their wives. Riding in her husband's private railroad car, she listened to strategy plans and gained firsthand knowledge of many aspects of running a nationwide political race.

Louis Howe was working with Franklin on this campaign, too, and Eleanor gradually overcame her initial dislike for the man. Howe tried to broaden Eleanor's political education by insisting that she read through Franklin's speeches. As she did so, she found that politics was a fascinating field, and her interest grew. Soon she was able to discuss intelligently a wide range of topics and issues.

All the political experts of the day predicted a defeat for the Democrats. Nonetheless, the team of Cox and Roosevelt fought a hard fight. The election in November proved the experts correct, however, and the Republicans won a landslide victory. Franklin, who had resigned as assistant secretary of the navy, returned to his law practice in New York City.

Back in New York once more, Eleanor decided to keep busy with something other than social teas and dinners. Always anxious to broaden her horizons and continually learn something new, she cast about for things to keep her occupied. One of the first things she did was to take a course in cooking. Because there had always been a cook on the household staff, she had never needed to learn how to work in a kitchen. Now,

at the age of thirty-six, she began learning what most women learn in their teens.

Since the cooking class alone did not take up all her time, Eleanor also enrolled in a business school where she studied typing and shorthand. Her mother-in-law was quite upset about all this, but Eleanor was determined to develop her own newfound individuality.

"I was thinking things out for myself," she wrote later. "Had I never done this, perhaps I might have saved some difficult experiences, but I have never regretted even my mistakes. They all added to my understanding of other human beings, and I came out in the end a more tolerant, understanding, and charitable person."

In the summer of 1921, the Roosevelt family went once again to Campobello. The days were filled with sailing and swimming and entertaining guests who came for visits. One afternoon in August, after taking a swim to cool off, Franklin complained of a chill and decided to go to bed without supper. The next day he felt even worse, and a day or so later he realized that his legs were becoming paralyzed. A local doctor was sent for, but he could not explain the illness, which at first he diagnosed as a common cold.

Days passed and Franklin showed no improvement. There were no nurses available, so Eleanor stayed with her husband day and night, sleeping on a cot nearby. When the ever-faithful Louis Howe arrived, he and Eleanor

The Roosevelt family in 1921. Front: Franklin, Jr., and John. Second row: Elliott, Anna, and James. Rear: Franklin, his mother Mrs. James Roosevelt, and Eleanor.

took turns rubbing Franklin's legs in an effort to restore feeling and circulation. At last a specialist was called from Newport, Rhode Island, who correctly diagnosed the illness as infantile paralysis.

"Will he recover?" asked the tired and anxious Eleanor.

The doctor was slow to answer the question. At last he turned to her and said, "You may as well know the truth. He might never walk again."

Many women would have crumpled at this startling news, but Eleanor Roosevelt was made of stern inner stuff despite her outward shyness and timidity. She made a pledge to devote herself entirely to helping him fight the dreaded disease.

Arrangements were made to take Franklin to a hospital in New York City. This required placing him in the bottom of a small boat and taking him to Eastport, Maine, where, on his stretcher, he was passed through the window of a train for the journey to New York. There he was taken to Presbyterian Hospital, where he remained until just before Christmas.

As Franklin Roosevelt began his long, slow fight to regain his health, a conflict ensued within the family. His mother was convinced that he would always be an invalid, and therefore wanted him to leave politics and business and retire to Hyde Park. Eleanor knew her husband better than his mother knew her son, however. She was convinced that the best therapy for Franklin was for him to retain his active interest in the world around him. His mother did not want him to have many visitors, especially political associates. Eleanor thought that visitors would be good for him. It became a personal struggle between the forceful mother-in-law and the quiet wife.

The two never engaged in an open struggle with harsh words and recriminations. Both women were well-bred and polite. But it was a silent tug-of-war between two strong-willed women, each of whom believed firmly that she was right. With supreme determination and the quiet assistance of Louis Howe, Eleanor won the battle. She stood by her husband as he worked to return to a normal life. The illness proved to be a turning point for the best in the lives of both Franklin and Eleanor Roosevelt.

The years passed slowly and Eleanor took on the additional burden of trying to be a father as well as a mother to her children. Franklin could roll on the floor and play games with the younger children, but it fell to Eleanor to join in their outside activities. Soon she was learning to be a camper—pitching tents, paddling canoes, building campfires, and learning to fish. She also took up horseback riding again and learned to swim.

Eleanor also kept the Roosevelt name in the political arena of New York. With two friends, Marion Dickerman and Nancy Cook, she helped organize the Democratic women in New York State. She helped raise funds for the women's division of the Democratic State Committee and was the editor of the *Women's Democratic News*. She also made her first political speech at a luncheon.

With each new field she entered, Eleanor seemed to gain the confidence to try yet another. In 1926 she and her friends, Miss Cook and Miss Dickerman, started a furniture factory at Hyde Park to provide employment for local farmers. The factory turned out some excellent reproductions of early colonial furniture. In 1927, Eleanor and her friends purchased the Todhunter School for Girls in New York City. Eleanor became a teacher of English, American history, and literature.

The year 1928, however, marked the greatest turning point in the life of Eleanor Roosevelt since Franklin had been stricken with polio in 1921. In this year, Franklin was nominated for governor of New York on the Democratic ticket. He won the election handily and Eleanor now found herself in a new role—that of the First Lady of New York State.

Eleanor camping with her children. Since Franklin was unable to engage in strenuous physical movement, Eleanor learned to join in this kind of outside activity.

First Lady of the Nation

The years as the governor's lady at Albany proved to be an invaluable experience for Eleanor Roosevelt. She learned a great many things which would serve her well in future years as America's first lady. Beginning in January of 1929, when Franklin was inaugurated governor, Eleanor became her husband's legs, eyes, and ears.

Every official who is responsible for institutions or departments must, in order to do his or her job properly, become familiar with the day-to-day workings of these institutions. Though Franklin had progressed well along the recovery trail and had regained complete use of his hands and arms, he could not walk without the use of crutches or a cane and someone's arm.

Therefore, the Governor instructed his wife on how to inspect properly the inside of various departments and state buildings while he was being driven around the grounds.

"At first my reports were highly unsatisfactory to him," Eleanor remembered later. "I would tell him what was on the menu for the day and he would ask: 'Did you look to see whether the inmates were actually getting that food?' I learned to look into the cooking pots on the stove and to find out if the contents corresponded to the menu. I learned to notice whether the beds were too close together, and whether they were folded up and put into closets or behind doors during the day, which would indicate that they filled the corri-

dors at night! I learned to watch the patients' attitude toward the staff and before the end of our years in Albany, I had become a fairly expert reporter on state institutions."

Eleanor not only served as a very active governor's wife but continued her teaching duties at the Todhunter School which she enjoyed immensely, and kept up her work with the state Democratic women's organizations. Of course, she also was still the mother of five children, though in 1929 the last child, John, was sent off to boarding school along with the others. Her summers and holidays, though, were devoted to her children and one year she took her two youngest boys for a grand tour of Europe.

In the political campaign of 1930, the year following the crash of the Wall Street stock market, Franklin ran for re-election as governor of New York. This time he won by a landslide. No Democrat had ever amassed so large a vote in a gubernatorial election.

Franklin was also gaining national prominence as he attended numerous governors' conferences in various states across the country. Eleanor often went along and came to meet many other governors' wives and the wives of Democratic chairmen and officials. Murmurs about the possibility of Franklin becoming a presidential candidate in 1932 began to grow. He certainly appeared to be the greatest Democratic vote-getter in the country.

When the Democratic National Convention met in Chicago in June, 1932, the United States was already deep into economic depression. Thousands had lost all their savings in the stock

Left, Franklin Delano Roosevelt is the Democratic party's presidential nominee in 1932, at a time when the country was deep into an economic depression. Above, Franklin takes the oath of office of the presidency, March 4, 1933.

market and millions were without jobs, and any man with whom the Democrats could hope to win the presidency had to be one who could offer hope of relief from the chaos that gripped America. The Democrats chose as their candidate Franklin Roosevelt, who though he was handicapped had proven to be an efficient and practical governor of the state of New York.

In November of that year, Franklin Delano Roosevelt was elected by a landslide over the Republican incumbent, Herbert Hoover. At his inauguration on March 4, 1933, he told the nation, "the only thing we have to fear is fear itself." People listened and gained hope from the obvious courage of a man who had assumed the burden of the presidency at such an awful time in America's history. The nation also took its first look at the quiet, slender woman who stood by his side.

Traditionally, the wife of the president did little more than play hostess to visiting dignitaries, arrange formal dinners and informal luncheons and teas, occasionally launch a ship, and in general stay in the background. This was definitely not Eleanor Roosevelt's style. In the years that her husband had been in the public eye, she had grown used to being active, rather than acting as an honorary participant in events. She preferred meeting people on a person-to-person basis rather than with pomp and formality. But she also recognized the need for a certain amount of protocol and ceremony. ". . . until I learned that it was really required for two purposes—protection and orderly procedure—I resented it deeply, as do most Americans." Mrs. Helm, who became the Roosevelts' social secretary, handled most of the affairs of protocol with occasional assistance from the State Department.

The very nature of the Roosevelt clan often reduced formality to a shambles. Some of the children were married now and others were away at school, but the White House was "home" for family gatherings on holidays and vacations. Valuable antiques were moved out of the family areas of the White House because when the Roosevelt boys got together, there was usually a lot of horseplay and roughhousing. This came as somewhat of a shock to the staid White House staff, but they soon became accustomed to the boisterous Roosevelts.

Eleanor in particular surprised the staff. Despite her obvious culture and well-bred background, she liked to do things for herself. Never before had anyone seen a first lady moving and rearranging furniture while butlers stood by in stunned amazement. Never before had a president's wife run the elevator by herself. Some Sunday mornings, she could be found in the kitchen happily frying eggs and bacon for her family. First ladies always rode in the White House limousine, even to destinations only a couple of blocks away. Not Eleanor! She enjoyed walking and refused to follow the old tradition of riding everywhere.

Soon after the Roosevelts moved into the White House in 1933, Miss Malvina "Tommy" Thompson came to work full time as Eleanor's secretary. She had been with Eleanor on a part-time basis since 1922 and the two women were close personal friends until Tommy's death many years later.

Franklin Roosevelt had to rely on advisers for any appraisal of conditions around the country, since it takes time before governmental programs begin to show their effect. Some of these advisers, however, were simply "yes-men" who always told the President what they thought he wanted to hear. He felt he could get the truest picture from his wife, and sent Eleanor out many times to gather information and report conditions directly to him.

The experience she had gained while Franklin was governor of New York served her well at this task. She had a basic need to satisfy her curiosity about many things, and soon the nation was astounded at the travels and activities of this unusual First Lady. Perhaps the most noted of these was the first time she donned a miner's lantern-cap and journeyed to the depths of a coal mine. Another time she invited some congressmen and their wives to lunch—and then took them on a tour of slum areas within

As First Lady, Eleanor often broke many precedents. Above, she wears a miner's cap and visits a coal mine. Below, she gives a radio broadcast, a task which always terrified her.

sight of the Capitol building in Washington, D.C. This helped to attain congressional support for slum clearance and housing development. She helped serve soup to the unemployed in the food lines, inspected hospitals and work camps, and toured the shantytowns of Puerto Rico and Appalachia. There seemed to be no place where she might not pop in unexpectedly.

Each time she returned from one of these trips, she and Franklin would dine together alone and Eleanor would deliver her report. The President would interrupt often to ask specific and penetrating questions. Sometimes his wife had ideas for solutions to problems and the President listened with interest and respect. He could not always comply with her plans and wishes, but he always carefully considered all she had to say. After Louis Howe's death in 1936, Franklin turned even more to rely on Eleanor, for Howe had been the President's closest adviser.

Eleanor's own personal endeavors also occupied a great deal of her time. Beginning in January, 1936, she wrote a daily syndicated newspaper column called "My Day." This was written in the fashion of a diary of her life as the First Lady. During her early years in the White House, she traveled more than a quarter of a million miles on lecture tours to all corners of America. She also delivered many radio speeches. These to her were the most terrifying of all her duties. She took lessons in speech and breath control, however, and in time became an excellent radio speaker. All of these activities were in addition to her regular duties as first lady. In her private work, she earned more than half a million dollars—all of which was donated to charity.

Another Eleanor Roosevelt innovation at the White House was her weekly news conference. She had a great affection for the press—especially the women reporters—and they returned the affection. At first, she refused to discuss political issues, but later Franklin found her press conferences a handy means of "sending up a trial balloon." Eleanor would comment about a particular issue as if she were expressing her own ideas. Franklin would then watch public reaction to his wife's comments and use this as a guide for his own actions. Only women reporters were allowed to attend

Top, Eleanor addresses the National Women's Committee of the Mobilization for Human Needs, of which she is chairman (1935). Bottom, Eleanor and Franklin arriving at a dinner given by the Cabinet. This dinner honored the third anniversary of Franklin's inauguration as president.

her own press conferences, and she saw to it that they were on equal terms with the men at presidential press conferences. In this way she did much to assure the women reporters their jobs during the depression. Occasionally she gave the women a "scoop," the earliest information of a particularly newsworthy event. She never let them scoop one another, however; they all got the same information at the same time.

The White House frequently receives many high-ranking foreign visitors, including diplomats and royal families. In the summer of 1939, the King and Queen of England arrived in America for a visit. Here Eleanor was at her best as a hostess. The nations of Europe were expecting war at almost any moment, and it was felt that a visit from the royal family would help cement good relations between Britain and America. In a second world war, close ties with England and the British Empire would be necessary.

During their stay in Washington, King George VI and Queen Mary were taken on a tour of the city, including a visit to George Washington's home, Mount Vernon. Later Franklin and Eleanor invited the royal couple to Hyde Park for an informal picnic. The people in charge of protocol were astounded to find that Eleanor had planned a completely American meal with no frills, including hot dogs, baked beans, smoked turkey, and strawberry shortcake. Franklin and the King also took a dip in the pool. When the royal train pulled out of the station at Hyde Park that evening, Franklin and Eleanor stood in the crowd and sang "Auld Lang Syne." Both couples felt that a

new and stronger bond of friendship now existed between the two great nations.

Two of Eleanor's greatest personal interests were minority groups and the youth of America. She had long been an enemy of discrimination whether class, racial, or religious. Now, as first lady of the land, she could exert more influence in trying to remedy the grievances of these groups. She could not command that anything be done, of course, but gentle and persistent persuasion from the president's wife could not easily be denied. When an occasion arose which especially upset her, she could take swift action to demonstrate her beliefs. When the Daughters of the American Revolution refused to allow the great Negro singer, Marian Anderson, to perform at Constitution Hall, Eleanor quickly invited Miss Anderson to sing at the White House.

Eleanor was very much concerned about the youth of America. During the depression years, numerous programs were initiated by the President to assist the jobless. This group of programs was known as the New Deal. Most of the government's money was spent to aid the breadwinner of the family. Eleanor felt that young people and students also should be given assistance to continue their studies or to learn new vocations and skills. She invited youth groups to the White House to talk about their problems and she worked closely with various youth organizations to improve the lot of the youth of the United States. She was instrumental in the creation of the National Youth Administration (NYA) in 1935. The NYA provided employ-

Eleanor holding a press conference. Only women reporters were permitted at her press conferences, and often she gave them early information, or "scoops," on important news stories.

ment for persons between the ages of sixteen and twenty-five, and part-time employment for needy high school, college, and graduate students.

"I believed, of course, that these young people had the right to be heard," Eleanor wrote later. "It was essential to restore their faith in the power of democracy to meet their needs, or they would take the natural path of looking elsewhere."

In September, 1939, war broke out in Europe as Adolf Hitler launched an attack upon Poland. Here in America, most sympathies were with the British and French who went, too late, to Poland's aid. But there was also a tremendous anti-war movement and an isolationist attitude. President Roosevelt was now faced with the problem of trying to keep America out of the war and at the same time to coax defense appropriations from a reluctant Congress.

Meanwhile, the war spread across Europe. Poland fell, and the Netherlands, Belgium, France, Denmark, and Norway followed in short order. Next, Hitler turned his armies upon Yugoslavia and Greece. Fighting raged in the Libyan Desert and then the Nazis swarmed across Russia. Britain was fighting for its very existence against the Germans, who were using U-boats to prevent neutral ships carrying food to pass their blockade. The people of the British Isles were threatened with starvation. America lent its aid as best it could, short of declaring war.

Eleanor remembered Franklin telling her in August, 1941, that "he was going to take a little trip up through the Cape Cod Canal and that he wished

to do some fishing. Then he smiled and I knew he was not telling me all that he was going to do. I had already learned never to ask questions when information was not volunteered." The President actually went away to Argentia, Newfoundland, for a top-secret meeting with Prime Minister Churchill. Both Elliott, now in the air corps, and Franklin, Jr., who was a naval officer, joined their father at that historic meeting, but Eleanor did not learn where they had been until Franklin's return to Washington.

In September of 1941, the Roosevelts experienced a sad double personal loss. Franklin's mother and Eleanor's younger brother Josh died within three weeks of each other. Sara Roosevelt was buried on her estate at Hyde Park and Josh was laid to rest at Tivoli where he and Eleanor had spent so much of their childhood.

No one could have guessed at that moment that national tragedy would occur three short months later. Tragic world events brought Winston Churchill back to the White House for Christmas of 1941. On December 7, 1941—a "day of infamy" Franklin Roosevelt called it—the Japanese attacked American military bases at Pearl Harbor in Hawaii.

America was now at war, and once again life in Washington, D.C., would move at a hectic pace. Tremendous new demands would be placed on all public servants as the United States prepared to fight a global war. The President would have to bear the greatest burden of them all. Now, more than ever, he would need the assistance of his wife, who served as his eyes, ears, and legs. Eleanor Roosevelt would meet the challenge.

Far left, top: Eleanor addresses the Democratic National Convention in 1940. Behind her is Alben W. Barkley. Bottom: FDR votes at Hyde Park in 1940. Left to right, Eleanor, Franklin's mother, Franklin, and Thomas Qualters, a Roosevelt aide.

At the Democratic National Convention in 1940, President Roosevelt was renominated for an unprecedented third term. John Nance Garner, the Texan who had been Mr. Roosevelt's vice-president for the past eight years, was not running again. The convention would have to nominate someone else. There were any number of nominees, each with a host of supporters, and the convention soon became bogged down in a wild melee. Mr. Roosevelt had hoped that Henry Wallace, the secretary of agriculture, would be nominated, but in all the confusion anything could happen. It is essential that the vice-president be a person who can work closely with the president and carry out his policies in the event something should happen to the president. Mr. Roosevelt decided that Henry Wallace was just such a man.

Mrs. Roosevelt was called at her home in Hyde Park and asked to go to Chicago, site of the convention, to help straighten things out. She had dedicated her life to assisting her husband and so without a moment's hesitation, she boarded a private plane and flew to Chicago.

The hall was a pandemonium. Delegations were marching up and down, bands were blaring, and speakers were trying to restore order. Mrs. Roosevelt was doubtful that she would even be heard but when she was introduced the hall became completely silent.

Mrs. Roosevelt was a little bit frightened as she started out into the sweltering, smoked-filled hall. She began to talk quietly and calmly into the microphone, explaining why her husband wanted Mr. Wallace.

When she was through, she thanked the delegates for their attention and quietly left the speakers stand. For a long moment there was only silence. Then the organ struck up "God Bless America" and a thunderous ovation rocked the convention hall. The balloting then began and Henry Wallace was nominated.

Mrs. Roosevelt rode back to the airport and her plane was taxiing out to the runway when it was suddenly called back. The President wanted her on the telephone. He had listened to her speech on the radio and wanted to tell her she had done a good job. Once more she had served her husband well.

First Lady of the World

The nation was shocked and angered by the sneak attack at Pearl Harbor, and many panicky rumors started. One particularly frightening rumor was that the Japanese were going to attack the west coast of the United States. Blackout regulations immediately went into effect and air raid wardens walked their beats that first night after the attack at Pearl Harbor. The following day, however, the nation had cause to refute the rumors of invasion or air attack. Eleanor Roosevelt arrived in California as assistant director of the Office of Civilian Defense (OCD). Surely, the people said, the President would not allow his wife to go there if danger were imminent. The blackouts continued for many months as a security measure, but the rumors stopped and most people forgot their fears.

Eleanor made the trip to California with the director of the OCD, Mayor Fiorello LaGuardia of New York. During her trip, she journeyed up the entire west coast of the United States from San Diego, California, to Seattle, Washington. Eleanor did not receive pay for this work, nor was she even paid expenses. Still, members of Congress who opposed her husband's policies criticized her efforts and made slanderous remarks. She was used to this type of thing, however, and accepted it with quiet dignity.

"All people in public life are subject to this type of slander," she once wrote. "A man who chooses to hold public office must learn to accept the slander as part of the job and to trust that the majority of the people will judge him by his accomplishments in the public service. A man's family also has to learn to accept it."

In February of 1942, Eleanor resigned from the OCD. "I did not much

Eleanor waits in a chow line with the soldiers during her visit to the South Pacific area. She made it a point to speak to as many enlisted men as possible, in order to raise the morale among the fighting men.

mind what they said about me," she said, "but when I found that anyone I appointed was in trouble merely because I appointed him, I did mind."

With America now in the war, many world leaders came to visit the White House to seek assistance or to make plans for war operations. Besides Winston Churchill, there were also Madame Chiang Kai-shek of China, Queen Wilhelmina of Holland, Crown Princess Marta of Norway, Prime Minister Mackenzie King of Canada, and numerous others. Eleanor received them all graciously and tried to make them feel at home in the White House.

Late in 1942, the President asked Eleanor to go to England for a visit. He hoped that Eleanor's presence would help boost the morale of American servicemen stationed in Great Britain. This would also give Eleanor a chance to inspect the work that women were doing in the war effort there. There was another reason, too: the duties of the presidency were so demanding that they made it almost impossible for Franklin to get away for very long except on matters of the utmost urgency. As Churchill's visit to the United States had pointed up the close relationship of the two countries, so Eleanor's trip would demonstrate the solidarity of the friendship. Her faithful secretary Tommy Thompson accompanied her on this mission.

In England, she was greeted by the King and Queen and visited with them at Buckingham Palace. Later they took Eleanor on a tour of the bombed areas of London. They stood on the steps of the great old St. Paul's Cathedral, designed by Christopher Wren and completed in 1711, and she saw the terrible devastation which spread for blocks and blocks in all directions. Miraculously, the famous cathedral had escaped serious damage.

From London, Eleanor went to Chequers, the country estate for British prime ministers, where she visited with Mr. Churchill and his lovely wife, Clementine. Mrs. Churchill took Eleanor on tours of hospitals, airfields, factories, and even anti-aircraft positions—all of which were covered by women. Eleanor

Top, Eleanor reviews a group of ferry pilots, many of them American, at an Air Transport Auxiliary Airfield during her tour of England in 1942. Bottom, Eleanor chats with her son Elliott, who was a Lieutenant Colonel during World War II.

was convinced that American women could play as important a part in the war effort as their British counterparts were doing.

One of the prime objectives of the trip was to visit with American servicemen stationed at various camps throughout Great Britain. Eleanor talked with flight crews of B-17 Flying Fortresses who were making daily strikes at Nazi targets. She talked with infantry regiments and Ranger battalions. Everywhere she went she collected the names and addresses of servicemen's families, to whom she would write letters when she returned to America.

For security reasons, Eleanor was given the secret code-name of "Rover" for her travels abroad. The President was kept informed of "Rover's" whereabouts at all times. When it came time for Eleanor to return to the United States, there was some discussion as to how she should travel. Mr. Roosevelt, who missed his wife very much, finally sent an order which said: "I don't care how you send her home, just send her!"

In the summer of 1943, Eleanor finally received the President's permission to make a trip to the South Pacific area. Mr. Norman Davis, the chairman of the American Red Cross, asked Eleanor to inspect the many Red Cross installations scattered throughout the area she planned to visit. Accordingly, Eleanor wore a Red Cross uniform throughout her trip.

On this trip, she visited dozens of places including New Zealand, Australia, New Caledonia, and tiny Christmas Island. At each place, she talked with American servicemen and, as she had done in Great Britain, collected names and addresses of their families back home. On the recommendation of her sons, all now commissioned officers in the service, she spent as much time as she could with the enlisted men. Battle-worn soldiers and marines could hardly believe their eyes when they found her standing in the chow lines at six o'clock in the morning. One young soldier stopped dead in his tracks just a few feet away, stared in amazement, and

Top: Eleanor (left) and the wife of General Douglas MacArthur chat in Australia, during Eleanor's tour of the South Pacific area. Bottom: VIPs attend a $100-a-plate dinner on Washington's Birthday in 1943, in support of the Democratic party.

then exploded, "Gosh! It's Eleanor!" The First Lady laughed and said she accepted such familiarity as a compliment.

Admiral Halsey, commander of the navy's Third Fleet, gave Eleanor permission to visit Guadalcanal in the Solomon Islands. Here, several months before, the United States Marines had begun the first major American offensive action in the Pacific. Eleanor was impressed with the little church in the American military cemetery which had been built by the natives of Guadalcanal. During her stay there, she even had to take cover once in a shelter when an air-raid alert sounded. After visiting Guadalcanal, she headed for home with a stop in Hawaii before going on to California.

Of her trip, Eleanor was to write, "At first I could hardly bear the hospitals. . . . a horrible consciousness of waste and feeling of resentment . . . burned within me as I wondered why men could not sit down around a table and settle their differences before an infinite number of the youth of many nations had to suffer."

In March of 1944, Eleanor was off on another inspection tour for the President. This time she took Tommy with her on a 13,000-mile journey to the Caribbean area. The men stationed in that area were resentful of the fact that they could not get to the war fronts of the world. They were, however, doing a demanding and crucial job of guarding the tremendous amount of shipping in the Caribbean from U-boat attack. They had done their job so well that few U-boats dared venture into that area, and consequently there was now little action.

"Franklin wanted the men to realize," she wrote, "that he knew and understood the whole picture and believed they were doing a vital job—that they were not forgotten, even though they were not on the front line." Eleanor carried the President's message to the men.

Eleanor writing her syndicated column "My Day." She began writing this column in January, 1936, after her husband had been president for almost three years.

The year 1944 was an election year and Franklin D. Roosevelt decided to run for an unprecedented fourth term. He was tired and haggard and it was obvious that his health was failing. The strain of bearing the great burden of leading his nation through a terrible war was beginning to tell. Still, he felt he must see it through. He ran for re-election and defeated the Republican candidate, Thomas E. Dewey.

Eleanor recognized her husband's weakening physical condition and tried to coax him to slow down. The Allies were advancing on all fronts and the issue of who would win the war was no longer in doubt. But Franklin shared his wife's dream of a world organization devoted to peace and felt that now was the time to prepare the groundwork for the realization of such a plan after the war was ended. Early in 1945, he sailed off to Yalta, on the Black Sea, for another conference with Prime Minister Churchill and Premier Stalin of Russia. Upon his return to America, he addressed the Congress and then went away to his health resort in Warm Springs, Georgia. Eleanor never saw her husband alive again. On April 12, 1945, Franklin Delano Roosevelt died of a cerebral hemorrhage.

Of their marriage, Eleanor was to write: "Men and women who live together through long years get to know one another's failings; but they also come to know what is worthy of respect and admiration in those they live with and in themselves. If at the end one can say, 'This man used to the limit the powers that God granted him; he was worthy of love and respect and of the sacrifices of many people, made in order that he might achieve what he deemed to be his task,' then that life has been lived well and there are no regrets."

Vice-President Harry S. Truman assumed the tremendous burden of the presidency and Eleanor moved out of the White House to an apartment in Washington Square in New York City. She was now alone and on her own.

Eleanor had to make a decision. "I could live on what my husband had left me and stop working. Or I could continue to work and pay most of what I earned to the government in taxes. I don't suppose that there was really much of a decision to make because, of course, I wanted to go on working."

During the last seventeen years of her life, Eleanor Roosevelt interviewed, visited, entertained, or chatted with most of the world's leaders. In England,

she visited with the Churchills and the royal family and unveiled a statue of her late husband in London's Grosvenor Square. She visited the tiny Dutch Island of Tholen where the founder of the American Roosevelt family had once lived, and she was greeted by Queen Juliana. She talked to the Russian dictator, Nikita Khrushchev, near Yalta, and visited with Prime Minister Nehru in New Delhi, India.

All of her time was not spent in the company of world leaders, however. She continued to write her column "My Day" and to make appearances on television and radio. Her interest in young people never waned and she was happy for the chance to read manuscripts for the Junior Literary Guild and to recommend those she felt youngsters would most enjoy. Other than her United Nations work, most of her time was taken by her lecture tours. She seemed almost tireless in her travels around the United States and the world.

Eleanor Roosevelt was interested in the common people of other lands— shepherds, miners, teachers, fishermen, and factory workers. She retained her intense curiosity about working conditions, living conditions, what people ate, how much they were paid, their educa-

tion, and their health. She wrote and lectured about the things she saw and thus focused attention on true conditions.

She was especially popular with children wherever she went. Little Israeli refugees, Swedish orphans, crippled Japanese children—all of them flocked around her with the instinctive love children have for people they know are kind. Negroes, Orientals, Catholics, Jews, Buddhists—all races and religions —accepted her as a kindly and gracious "grandmother" who told them stories and listened to them with real interest.

While Eleanor was a delegate to the United Nations, she did not feel that she should become involved in American politics. She did, however, support President Truman's bid for re-election in 1948, and he once even said he would be happy to have her as his vice-presidential candidate! In 1952, she supported Adlai Stevenson, but did not campaign actively. The presidential campaign of 1956, however, was a different story, since she was no longer involved directly with the United Nations. Mr. Stevenson, who had served with Mrs. Roosevelt in the United Nations, was nominated once again. This time the former First Lady undertook a very

Top left, Eleanor addresses the Democratic National Convention in 1960 on behalf of Adlai Stevenson. Bottom, Eleanor with John Fitzgerald Kennedy, for whom she campaigned in the 1960 election. Above, she is shown campaigning for Kennedy.

strenuous campaign in Mr. Stevenson's behalf. President Eisenhower was re-elected, but Mrs. Roosevelt had done her best. In 1960, her last political campaign, Mrs. Roosevelt traveled the country making speeches in behalf of Senator John F. Kennedy.

President Kennedy re-appointed her to the United Nations, and Mrs. Roosevelt was thrust once again before the eyes of the world. The organization was honored by her presence and the hostilities of many nations toward the American delegation seemed to diminish.

The many years of hard work were beginning to take their toll. She grew a little stooped, walked a little more slowly, and gradually began reducing her work load. More and more she liked to gather her children, grandchildren, and great-grandchildren about her. Each summer there were many hot dog roasts and picnics at her cottage at Hyde Park.

Illness at last overtook the grand and gracious woman who now was referred to by many as the First Lady of the World. In July, 1962, she was carried to the hospital. Prayers were offered all over the world for her recovery, and for a time she seemed to improve. She went back to Campobello for what she knew would be the last visit, and then back to New York where she suffered other setbacks. On November 7, 1962, Eleanor Roosevelt died.

The world mourned the loss of its first lady. Great personages from all around the world gathered as she was laid to rest beside her husband in the rose garden at Hyde Park. Countless millions prayed at shrines, churches, and synagogues as they remembered her devotion to the cause of human rights and human welfare. It was her destiny to create hope, faith, and understanding among all men. Many times she fought alone against suffering and deprivation, but she never lost her belief in the brotherhood of man. Perhaps her philosophy of life was best expressed by Adlai Stevenson when he said, "She would rather light one little candle than curse the darkness."

Summary

In her youth, Eleanor Roosevelt might have been categorized as a "poor little rich girl." Born into a wealthy family, she was never to know a day of hunger or anything but a handsome, comfortable home. She was very rich in the material things of life, and might easily have squandered away her life in the indolent luxury of old New York's high society.

But Eleanor Roosevelt was also poor, in a sense. She was starved for love and affection. She was orphaned at the age of ten and had never really had a true family life prior to that. Deprived of parental guidance and security, she developed many fears and anxieties. For many years as a child, she withdrew into a shell, a dreamworld, quite apart from the realities of the life she was living. Anxious to please her relatives and so win their affection, she became afraid to act on her own lest she make a mistake.

For one reason, and for one reason alone, Eleanor found she could brush aside her fears and face life as it really existed. That reason was service to others. From adolescence, she seemed to have an instinctive compassion for her fellow human beings. Within her own strata of society, there were few who needed help. And so, with supreme determination, she mustered her courage, quelled her fears, and went instead to help in the Bowery and Hell's Kitchen.

Her greatest challenge came when her husband was stricken with polio. This, of course, was a more personal interest. Believing as she did, however, in her husband's destiny to be in public service, this job was given a greater depth of meaning. She would help Franklin Delano Roosevelt bring a "New Deal" to America in its time of poverty, starvation, and depression.

As America's first lady, she cast aside old traditions and became her husband's ears, eyes, and legs. Whereas other first ladies had tended strictly to social activities in the White House, Mrs. Roosevelt journeyed out to meet the people. By her visits, sharecroppers, miners, farmers, slum dwellers, and hospital patients all felt they had direct communication with the White House. At last someone in Washington was taking a genuine interest in their affairs. Minority groups now found they had a powerful champion who cared.

After the death of her husband, Mrs. Roosevelt broadened her area of interest and concern. In the world forum of the United Nations organization she championed the cause of human rights for people the world over. A tireless traveler with an unceasing curiosity, she came to know and understand conditions in many nations besides her own. She devoted several decades of her life to the fight against deprivation and persecution.

Though she was not a woman of great physical beauty, she glowed with an inner beauty that revealed the compassion and love that made her, in the eyes of millions, the First Lady of the World.

Bibliography

ADAMIC, LOUIS. *Dinner at the White House.* New York: Harper & Brothers, 1946.

BELLUSH, BERNARD. *Franklin D. Roosevelt as Governor of New York.* New York: Columbia University Press, 1955.

BLACK, RUBY. *Eleanor Roosevelt: A Biography.* New York: Duell, Sloan & Pearce, 1940.

BOOTH, EDWARD TOWNSEND. *Country Life in America as Lived by Ten Presidents.* New York: Alfred A. Knopf, 1947.

BURNS, JAMES MACGREGOR. *Roosevelt: The Lion and the Fox.* New York: Harcourt, Brace and Company, 1956.

BYRNES, JAMES F. *Speaking Frankly.* New York: Harper & Brothers, 1947.

CARMICHAEL, DONALD SCOTT (ed.). *F.D.R., Columnist.* New York: Pelligrini & Cudahy, 1947.

CHURCHILL, WINSTON S. *The Gathering Storm.* Boston: Houghton Mifflin Company, 1948.

DANIELS, JONATHAN. *Frontier on the Potomac.* New York: The Macmillan Company, 1946.

———. *The End of Innocence.* Philadelphia: J. B. Lippincott Company, 1954.

DEAN, VERA. *Four Cornerstones of Peace.* New York: McGraw-Hill Book Company, 1946.

DOWS, OLIN. *Franklin Roosevelt at Hyde Park.* American Artist Group, 1949.

EATON, JEAN. *The Story of Eleanor Roosevelt.* New York: William Morrow and Company, 1956.

EICHELBERGER, CLARK. *U.N.: The First Ten Years.* New York: Harper & Brothers, 1955.

FARLEY, JAMES A. *Jim Farley's Story: the Roosevelt Years.* New York: McGraw-Hill Book Company, 1948.

FLYNN, EDWARD J. *You're the Boss.* New York: The Viking Press, 1947.

FORRESTAL, JAMES and WALKER MILLER. *Forrestal Diaries,* 1951.

FRIEDEL, FRANK. *Franklin D. Roosevelt,* 3 vols. Boston: Little, Brown and Company, 1952-1956.

FURMAN, BESS. *Washington By-Line,* 1949.

GRAFF, ROBERT and ROBERT EMMA GINNA, with text by ROGER BUTTERFIELD. *F.D.R.* New York: Harper & Row, 1963.

GUNTHER, JOHN. *Roosevelt in Retrospect.* New York: Harper & Brothers, 1950.

HAGEDORN, HERMANN. *The Roosevelt Family of Sagamore Hill,* 1954.

HATCH, ALDEN. *Franklin D. Roosevelt.* New York: Henry Holt and Company, 1947.

———. *Citizen of the World,* 1948.

HARRITY, RICHARD and RALPH MARTIN. *The Human Side of F.D.R.* New York: Duell, Sloan and Pearce, 1960.

HICKOK, LORENA. *Reluctant First Lady.* New York: Dodd, Mead & Company, 1962.

HOOVER, HERBERT C. *Memoirs,* 3 vols., 1951-1952.

HOOVER, IRVIN HOOD. *Forty-two Years in the White House.* Boston: Houghton Mifflin Company, 1934.

HULL, CORDELL. *Memoirs,* 2 vols. New York: The Macmillan Company, 1948.

HURD, CHARLES. *When the New Deal Was Young and Gay.* New York: Hawthorn Books, Inc., 1965.

ICKES, HAROLD L. *The Autobiography of a Curmudgeon.* New York: Reynal & Hitchcock, 1948.

———. *Secret Diary of Harold Ickes.* New York: Simon and Schuster, 1953.

LASH, JOSEPH. *Eleanor Roosevelt: A Friend's Memoir.* New York: Doubleday & Company, Inc., 1964.

LIE, TRYGVE. *Peace on Earth.* New York: Hermitage House, 1949.

McIntire, Ross T. *White House Physician.* New York: G. P. Putnam's Sons, 1946.

Moscow, Warren. *Politics in the Empire State.* New York: Alfred A. Knopf, 1948.

Nesbitt, Henrietta. *White House Diary.* New York: Doubleday and Company, Inc., 1948.

Perkins, Frances. *The Roosevelt I Knew.* New York: The Viking Press, 1946.

Pringle, Henry F. *Theodore Roosevelt.* New York: Harcourt, Brace & Company, 1931.

Roosevelt, Eleanor. *It's Up To the Women.* New York: Frederick A. Stokes Company, 1933.

———. *This is My Story.* New York: Harper & Brothers, 1937.

———. *If You Ask Me.* New York: D. Appleton-Century Co., 1946.

———. *This I Remember.* New York: Harper & Brothers, 1949.

———. *Personal Recollections: Franklin D. Roosevelt and Hyde Park,* 1949.

———. *India and the Awakening East.* New York: Harper & Brothers, 1953.

———. *It Seems to Me,* 1954.

———. *You Learn by Living,* 1957.

———. *On My Own.* New York: Harper & Brothers, 1958.

———. *The Autobiography of Eleanor Roosevelt.* New York: Harper & Brothers, 1961.

Roosevelt, Eleanor with William De Witt. *U.N.: Today and Tomorrow,* 1953.

Roosevelt, Eleanor and Lorena Hickok. *Ladies of Courage,* 1954.

Roosevelt, Eleanor with Helen Ferris. *Partners: The United States and Youth,* 1960.

———. *Your Teens and Mine.* New York: Doubleday & Company, Inc., 1961.

Roosevelt, Elliott. *As He Saw It.* New York: Duell, Sloan & Pearce, 1946.

Roosevelt, Elliott (ed.). *F.D.R. His Personal Letters. Early Years.* New York: Duell, Sloan & Pearce, 1947.

———. *F.D.R. His Personal Letters. Vol. II, 1905–1928.* New York: Duell, Sloan & Pearce, 1948.

Roosevelt, Elliott and Eleanor Roosevelt. *Hunting Big Game In the Eighties,* 1933.

Roosevelt, Franklin D. *Looking Forward.* New York: John Day Co., 1933.

———. *On Our Way.* New York: John Day Co., 1934.

Roosevelt, G. Hall. *Odyssey of an American Family.* 1939.

Roosevelt, James and Sidney Shalett. *Affectionately, F.D.R.* New York: Harcourt, Brace & Company, 1959.

Roosevelt, Mrs. James as told to Isabel Leighton and Gabrielle Forbush. *My Boy Franklin.* New York: Crown Publishing, 1933.

Roosevelt, Theodore. *Autobiography,* 1913.

Roosevelt, Mrs. Theodore. *Day Before Yesterday.* New York: Doubleday & Company, Inc., 1959.

Rosenman, Samuel I. (ed.). *The Public Papers and Addresses of Franklin D. Roosevelt,* 13 vols. New York: Random House, 1938 (for the years 1928–1936); The Macmillan Co., 1941 (for the years 1937–1941); Harper & Brothers, 1950 (for the years 1941–1945).

Rosenman, Samuel I. *Working with Roosevelt.* New York: Harper & Brothers, 1952.

Schlesinger, Arthur, Jr. *The Age of Roosevelt.* 1957.

Schriftgiesser, Karl. *The Amazing Roosevelt Family 1613–1942.* New York: Wilfred Funk, 1942.

Sherwood, Robert E. *Roosevelt and Hopkins.* New York: Harper & Brothers, 1948.

Smith, Alfred. *Up To Now.* New York: The Viking Press, 1929.

Starling, Edmund. *Starling of The White House.* New York: Simon and Schuster, 1946.

Steinberg, Alfred. *Mrs. R.: The Life of Eleanor Roosevelt.* New York: G. P. Putnam's Sons, 1958.

Stiles, Lilah. *The Man Behind Roosevelt: The Story of Louis McHenry Howe.* New York: World Publishing Company, 1954.

Tugwell, Rexford Guy. *The Stricken Land.* New York: Doubleday & Company, 1947.

Tully, Grace. *F.D.R., My Boss.* New York: Charles Scribner's Sons, 1949.

Walker, Turnley. *Roosevelt and the Warm Springs Story.* New York: A. A. Wyn, Inc., 1953.

Weingast, David E. *Franklin D. Roosevelt: Man of Destiny.* New York: Julian Messner, 1952.

Wharton, Don (ed.). *The Roosevelt Omnibus.* New York: Alfred A. Knopf, 1934.

Whittelsey, C. B. *Roosevelt Genealogy, 1649–1902,* 1902.

Mrs. Roosevelt's columns for *McCalls, Woman's Home Companion, The Ladies' Home Journal,* and her syndicated *My Day* columns (from 1935 on), are also valuable, as are the F.D.R. papers and letters at the F.D.R. Library at Hyde Park, New York.

Numerous United Nations publications, published by the U.N. Dept. of Publications, are of value, too. These include the "Declaration of Human Rights," "Impact of the Universal Declaration of Human Rights" (1953), and the "Year Books" (1946–1953).

Index